TAKE BACK
WHAT THE
DEVIL STOLE

TAKE BACK
WHAT THE
DEVIL STOLE

AN AFRICAN AMERICAN
PROPHET'S ENCOUNTERS IN
THE SPIRIT WORLD

ONAJE X. O. WOODBINE

Columbia University Press   *New York*

Columbia University Press
Publishers Since 1893
New York   Chichester, West Sussex
cup.columbia.edu

The author wishes to acknowledge grant support from the Louisville Institute.

Library of Congress Cataloging-in-Publication Data
Names: Woodbine, Onaje X. O., author.
Title: Take back what the devil stole : An African American Prophet's
Encounters in the Spirit World / by Onaje X. O. Woodbine.
Description: New York : Columbia University Press, 2021. |
Includes bibliographical references and index.
Identifiers: LCCN 2020032459 (print) | LCCN 2020032460 (ebook) |
ISBN 9780231197168 (hardback) | ISBN 9780231197175 (pbk.) |
ISBN 9780231552028 (ebook)
Subjects: LCSH: Haskins, Donna. | Christianity and other religions—
African. | Afro-Caribbean cults. | African American women—Religion. |
Religious biography—Massachusetts—Boston. | Boston (Mass.)—
Religious life and customs.
Classification: LCC BR128.A16 W66 2021 (print) | LCC BR128.A16 (ebook) |
DDC 277.44/61083092 [B]—dc23
LC record available at https://lccn.loc.gov/2020032459
LC ebook record available at https://lccn.loc.gov/2020032460

COVER ART: Billie J / agencyrush.com

To my mother, Robin M. Offley
A ballerina without equal, who gifted me with the
power of imagination

And to Oluwatoyin Salau, warrior queen,
gone but not forgotten
#SayHerName

Imagination! *who can sing thy force?*
Or who describe the swiftness of thy course?
Soaring through air to find the bright abode,
Th' empyreal palace of the thund'ring God,
We on thy pinions can surpass the wind,
And leave the rolling universe behind:
From star to star the mental optics rove,
Measure the skies, and range the realms above.
There in one view we grasp the mighty whole,
Or with new worlds amaze th' unbounded soul.
. . . .
Such is thy pow'r, nor are thine orders vain,
O thou the leader of the mental train:
In full perfection all thy works are wrought,
And thine the sceptre o'er the realms of thought.
Before thy throne the subject-passions bow,
Of subject-passions sov'reign ruler thou;
At thy command joy rushes on the heart,
And through the glowing veins the spirits dart.

—Phillis Wheatley, "On Imagination,"
Poems on Various Subjects Religious and Moral (1773)

CONTENTS

III CHILD OF LIGHT

ACKNOWLEDGMENTS

Ms. Donna Haskins and I like to say that this is "our" book. But it would not have come into being without her fearless courage and spiritual genius. Donna dedicates her life story to her sister Evelyn Anderson, and she gives "all the Glory and Honor to my savior Jesus Christ." Donna's daughter Joy and her granddaughter Amber were also very giving of their time. Many of the names in this book have been replaced with pseudonyms.

I also give thanks to my mother, Robin M. Offley, who sacrificed more than I can ever know for me to live, and my grandmother, Elaine Bell, who put food on the table and wisdom in my ears. Ms. Wilson, Ms. Doris Barros, Ms. Nile, Ms. Andrea Major Herbert, thank you for being my surrogate mothers, protectors, and grandmothers.

I am indebted to mentors and scholars who have opened the way for me to contribute to the world of ideas. I will be forever grateful to Stephen Prothero and Walter Fluker for being in the right place at the right time. Other mentors who opened the way are Chris R. Schlauch, Rosanna Salcedo, Dwayne Tunstall, Emmett Price III, Chief Awodele Ifayemi, Linda Carter Griffith, Christopher Lehrich, Imani-Sheila Newsome-Camara, and Victor Kestenbaum. Many thanks as well for the expert guidance and sage advice of editor Wendy Lochner and the entire editorial team at Columbia University Press.

I am deeply appreciative of my friends and colleagues at American University who supported my research, including my graduate student research assistant Kendall Tate. Copyeditors Marisa Pagano and Anita O'Brien commented on the manuscript with expert precision, and the beautiful photographs in this book are by Meera Subramanian (except for chapter 10). I would also like to thank Marvin Barros Jr., Manny Wilson, Bokeem Woodbine, Russell Paulding, Adam Hayes, Maurice Anderson, André Holland, Jeffery Mayi, and Damon Harper for their unconditional support of my work.

Finally, I am grateful to my extraordinary partner, Folasade Woodbine. I could not have asked for a better half. My son, Sowande Woodbine, you are proof the world can heal itself. To my father, Robert J. Woodbine, and my grandfather, Leroy Bell, thank you for your guidance and wisdom. And to my daughter, Ewaoluwa Woodbine, this book is for you.

TAKE BACK
WHAT THE
DEVIL STOLE

INTRODUCTION

S itting on his opioid-addicted mother's couch, the tall, dark boy with the magnetic smile watched the stranger, Donna, in silence. "You want to play basketball again?" she asked, perched across from Jason, her eyes twinkling.

The boy was shocked. How did this older woman, a complete stranger, know about his hip surgery, which ended his short-lived college basketball career and, more important, the game that held his soul together on Boston's inner-city streets?

"Yeah, I want to play again," Jason answered.

"You will," said Donna. "Just not how you think. You gonna play professional [just not how you think]."

Jason's mother had asked Donna to come and bless her family's apartment, to rid the dark cracks and corners of what the older woman called demonic creatures, the ones that turned themselves into ordinary objects, such as an old book resting on a countertop or a dirty microwave perched in the kitchen, to escape notice by capable eyes. But Donna's true purpose that day was to speak life into Jason's heart, to offer a Black boy hope that he would again play the game he loved despite the damage done to his body and the dangers of his environment.

Jason called Donna on the telephone several nights later. "Jason, the Holy Spirit told me your hip should be feeling better. There's nothing wrong with your hip. Your hip should be fine. Have you tried to go on the court? Go on the court for an hour and when you come back, call me."

"Yeah," Jason countered, "but I can't jump, Donna. I can't play on one leg!"

"Go outside right now and play," she insisted, ignoring his incredulity. "Go to the gym and play and then you call me back, you hear?!"

Jason didn't know it at the time, but Donna's words had remarkable power. Whatever she willed into being was likely to happen. Like any prophet worth her salt, she had a tongue that could whip things into existence. "Alright," Jason returned, "but I'm telling you, I can't jump with just one leg."

Jason grabbed his basketball anyway and hustled over to the gym. As he walked onto the court, he focused on the orange rim holding the net and mustered the courage to limp toward the hoop, ball in hand. Leaping into the air, Jason reached upward, as far as his arms could go, before smashing the ball down against the side of the rim.

"Boing!" went the hoop, which, like the ball, never lied. The backboard, Jason's mirror, offered a stark view of himself above the rim—not as he wanted to be, but as he really was. Now, he was grounded below it in "broken spirits." After several more attempts at self-transcendence, Jason tried one more time, resolving to give every ounce of his being to the hoop, which had so often lessened the pain of his mother's drug addiction and the verbal abuse he received at home. He limped and leapt off the hardwood—this time, the ball crashing down through the net.

"Slam!" Jason's body fell to the baseline, limp, lying across the white line that marked the boundary. Sobbing uncontrollably, he exclaimed, "I did it!" and rushed home to call Donna.

"The Holy Spirit showed me that your hip was healed, Jason, but your mind was holding you back. God already made you perfect."

A FAITH OF HER OWN

I learned about Donna's gift to make things happen with her words, to transgress the boundaries of linear time, and to teleport to other dimensions from Jason, a young man with whom I became very close in the process of writing my first book, *Black Gods of the Asphalt*.[1] In that book, I learned that streetball serves as a lived religion among Boston's young Black men, who, in times of crisis, become choreographers of the basketball court, playing the game to express grief, generate hope, and create a sense of belonging. But in the process of writing *Black Gods*, I also discovered that the Black women in these young men's lives were often the ones most responsible for the theological ideas, symbols, and practices exercised on the court. Listening to Jason and other young men talk about the spiritual gifts of Black women ignited my interest to know more about these, often overlooked women, not simply as secondary characters in a predominately Black male story but as main protagonists asserting their worth through a lived religion all their own.

SIGNIFICANCE OF THE STUDY

Harvard historian David Hall made the concept of "lived religion" prominent with his edited collection of essays entitled *Lived Religion in America: Toward a History of Practice*.[2] Since then, leading sociologists have produced notable research expanding on the term in the field. An excellent example of this is Nancy

Ammerman's *Sacred Stories, Spiritual Tribes: Finding Religion in Everyday Life.*[3]

Building on Ammerman's work, I turn my attention in this book to the role of religion in the everyday life of Black women in Boston, exploring how an ordinary person such as Ms. Donna Haskins creates meaning to address the problems of inner-city life in places beyond the reach of established religious institutions and the theological doctrines on which they are founded. Scholars of lived religion acknowledge that religious phenomena, such as ritual practice, healing, astral flight, transcendent experience, spiritual warfare, prophecy, and prayer, occur in places and times that exist apart from the control of recognized experts and religious authorities.[4]

Ammerman's suggestion that the term "lived religion" centers the role of the body in the study of religion has also proven instructive for this book. Womanist scholars such as Emilie Townes, Delores Williams, and Katie Cannon have underscored the ways in which, in the United States, Black women's bodies are "contested terrain upon which and through which is built structures of domination but also frameworks of struggle and transformation."[5] For Townes, it is in this particularity of Black women's bodies that we come not only to witness a "hope for wholeness, but also to understand the ways in which age and body image, and a history that contains the ultimate mammy, the emasculating bitch, the tragic mulatta, the castrating matriarch, and the pickaninny continue to" constrain Black women's freedom.[6] In *Devil Stole*, I have taken Womanist methodological and epistemological concerns for the body seriously, centering the "radical particularity" of Ms. Donna Haskins's everyday life with the understanding that her experiences "cannot be told in a vacuum. It is a story that can only be understood in relation to other stories—this is the universal or the first dawning of it."[7]

In this telling, we see how a contemporary Black woman constructs ultimate meanings, often on the peripheries of social and political power.

For the first four decades of Donna's life, her body was marked by a sense of powerlessness, repeatedly reduced by the prevailing narratives and institutions that define the streets of Boston to pornotropic themes of Black women as "object, immoral, other, accessible, hyper, simultaneously titillating, and curious, and, coincidentally, cursed yet good/s worth selling/out and purchasing and/or destroying."[8] This "theft of the body," as Black feminist scholar Hortense J. Spillers refers to the cultural abduction of Black women's right to self-possession,[9] was prescribed by the prevailing narratives and institutions that define the streets of Boston, such as Donna's neighborhood schools; the Boston police force; government housing projects; heterosexual white, Black, and Latino men; and family members, so that the image of the "ho or whatever" became Donna's primary consciousness of herself—a mutilation of her inner life that nearly ended in suicide on multiple occasions.

At the age of forty-six, having tried and failed to kill herself for the fourth time, and now at her lowest point, Donna wakens to the feminist preaching of a Black Baptist minister and the strange voice of an invisible presence, who enjoins her to stand up to the face of evil. "In order for me to speak a truer word concerning myself," remarks Spillers, "I must strip down through layers of attenuated meanings, made an excess in time, over time, assigned by a particular historical order, and there await whatever marvels of my own inventiveness."[10] Here, Donna's metamorphosis from an "object of history" to a complex subject of freedom begins.[11] Through the marvels of her own inventiveness and from the safety of her Roxbury apartment, she becomes aware of an-other dimension, a nonmaterial world defined not, for once, by people's perceptions of her body. This parallel dimension is where Donna chooses to anchor her newfound identity and, most fascinating, is populated by a vast array of supernatural entities drawn from Catholic, Black Baptist, and Afro-Caribbean religious grammars.

For people of African descent in the United States, suggests historian of religion Charles H. Long, the bizarre experience of being descended from slaves in a society whose language and culture have been "opaque" to this community has induced a proclivity for the inexpressible—a strange openness to that which is extraordinarily unfamiliar.[12] This experience of the "wholly other," or the uncanny, "has no place in our schemes of reality but belongs to an absolutely different one."[13] Yet when a person is in the presence of this "wholly other," it has the power to grip the body and mind, triggering powerful emotions of dread and awe that totally reshape a person's orientation toward themselves and others. In all expressions of community and cultural life, Long remarks, including the blues and dance, an African American has had to "experience the truth of his negativity and at the same time transform and create *an-other* reality. Given the limitation imposed upon him, he created on the level of his religious consciousness."[14] In the pages that follow, we enter the creative religious consciousness of Ms. Donna Haskins. This is the story of her body, her haunted landscapes, and her other worlds as she negotiates the streets of one of American's most racially segregated cities.[15]

MEETING DONNA

When Jason first invited me to meet Donna, I was extremely nervous about visiting her apartment, both because it was adjacent to one of Roxbury's most notorious housing projects and because Jason described her as a woman who did not live "in this world" but had chosen to spend most of her time venturing into another, less tangible area. Although Donna might appear to be carrying the weight of the world as a Black woman living in abject poverty, Jason explained, in this unseen dimension she was as elusive as a ray of light. As we walked toward the old brick factory, which had been turned into an apartment building where Donna spent most of her time slipping off her flesh to enter this obscure dimension, I couldn't help but think about my former friend "Smiley," a young man from the notorious Heath Street Projects now plainly in view.

Smiley and I were bused to the same predominately white high school in the Boston suburb of Newton during the late 1990s, as part of a Massachusetts school desegregation program Bostonians called METCO.[16] The program aimed to help Black and Latinx youth escape the daily gun violence of Boston's inner-city streets yet, in practice, introduced us to more subtle, symbolic forms of racial violence. Each morning at around five o'clock, the yellow METCO school buses circled around our neighborhoods, passing the housing projects, liquor stores, and boarded-up buildings before hauling us out on hourlong drives past the manicured lawns, impressive homes, and private back-yards of our mostly white classmates. Once the buses pulled into the sprawling campuses of *their* schools, we became the "METCO kids," labeled as such by the suburban students and teachers who understood little of our world's dangers. Even then, I wondered why, in my school's population of around one thousand students, most METCO kids were tracked into the same classes, especially lower-level mathematics and sciences, throughout our high school years. It wasn't until I was a senior that I was told, when the lone Black math teacher pulled me aside, cursing under her breadth, "You shouldn't be in such a low-level math class, Onaje. You are one of the smartest kids here!" That year, she transferred me to her higher-level class and, when I excelled, pulled me aside again to say: "To tell you the truth, you shouldn't even be in my class!"

Most of the boys on the METCO bus, like Smiley and me, lived in Boston's inner-city neighborhoods, where it was almost impossible *not* to be in a gang unless you played basketball or possessed some other talent that gave you a "pass" in the eyes of the gang's shot-callers. Smiley didn't have a streetball pass, so, to survive, he carried a switchblade with him onto the METCO bus. At least then, after school, when he got back to Roxbury, he could defend himself. Compared to Smiley, I was fortunate. I was a rising basketball star, which meant I was one of the few Black boys who were visible to white students and the teachers at our affluent suburban school. I was the "exception," and I got a street pass from the gang members in inner-city Roxbury, too, because I could hoop out of my mind on our neighborhood playgrounds. Basketball was the bridge that allowed me to cross over from one dangerous world to another.

Now, years later, as I walked past Smiley's old Projects on my way to meet Donna, I realized how close I had come to being Smiley, a mere jump shot between our lives. One afternoon our stories nearly collided as we stepped off the after-school bus in Roxbury's Dudley Station. We had spent much of the day together and planned to walk to my apartment.

"Onaje!!!" an older ball player named Mark, whom I admired, yelled out from across the street, standing next to his old, beat-up car. "Yo, Onaje! Come here, bro! How you been? I haven't seen you in a minute! Come here, I got a message from your older brother, Bo. I just hung out with him in L.A.!" I told Smiley I'd be right back and crossed the street to Mark.

"Yo, I was just hanging out with your older brother in Cali, yo," Mark continued. "Yo, he wanted me to tell you what's up.

He's got a lot of love for you man. We were hanging out hard. I just wanted you to know."

"For real, that's dope," I responded, trying to conjure an image of my brother, whom I hadn't seen since I was two years old. "That's—"

"Oh, shit! Get in the car—now!" Mark screamed. I looked up, and throngs of people were running frantically across Dudley Station, where I had been standing only minutes before. There was Smiley, running toward me, faster than I have ever seen anyone run, his lips and cheeks trembling as he worked his biceps and pumped his short, stocky legs with every ounce of power he had. In his fist, he held the extended switchblade stained with fresh blood. Behind him, young boys raced after, their eyes burning with hatred. Quivering with fear, I jumped into Mark's car, and we drove off, first circling around the block to see if we could catch up with Smiley. We found him with handcuffs around his wrists and the flashing lights of the police cars surrounding his chasers.

Two minutes after I left Smiley, two boys from the Academy Homes Projects, a rival gang, attacked him. Smiley pulled out his knife, stabbed one and then fled for his life before the perpetually stationed police officers detained him. If Mark hadn't called to me from across the street, heaven knows what might have happened.

Years later, as I was finishing my book on streetball in Boston, I read a news report about a young man who had been discovered with his girlfriend, face down on his living room floor, bullet holes in both their heads, a throat cut, and a newborn baby crying on the bed. To my despair, the dead man was Smiley.

Graffiti is spray-painted on the wall between Smiley's old housing projects and Donna Haskins's apartment. It reads, "Where Are You Now?" And I honestly don't know, as Jason and

I approach Donna's door and press the buzzer. Boston's inner-city streets have a way of raising existential questions about one's time and place in the world.

The security door opens, and Jason and I walk down a long, dimly lit corridor toward Donna's apartment. As we near the front door, which is open, I can barely finish my question—"Should I take my shoes off?"—before an older woman with smiling eyes and a chestnut complexion stops me short: "Boy, please! Leave your shoes on!" Donna's one-bedroom apartment was spotless, a simple, brown wooden table placed near the center of an open living room bearing nothing but an upright white cross. Toward the back of the apartment, two small, mangled couches sat, the favorite nesting places of her beloved gray cat, who gnawed on the furniture fabric so often that foam was bursting from the seams. The worn cotton had lost much of its shiny beige luster and was now a musty gray, the discoloration most likely caused by the potion of holy water, holy oil, Florida water, apple-cider vinegar, and alcohol Donna mixed together to spray on her furniture to dissuade demonic entities from lounging around her living room. Sage incense, frankincense, and myrrh, which she burned to stave off demonic attacks, wafted through the sweet-smelling air. And in her bedroom—her "war room"—Donna kept a shrine, a hidden spiritual chamber where, I later learned, she went to conduct spiritual warfare on behalf of people on the margins of history, like herself.

Donna's body, like her apartment, was a temple of modesty shrouding bruises and secrets. She donned a simple white blouse and long, flowing white skirt, her long shirtsleeves hiding the large skin abrasions she had received, she said, from her many encounters with evil. Her caramel face was soft and beautifully bare, and her fox-silver-colored hair created whatever shape it desired. The vanities of the salon were nothing to a woman who had already reclaimed her desire from the world. Donna's real beauty lay in another dimension, and according to her, in that spirit world, she was absolutely stunning. To give me a metaphor for the grandiosity of her inner life, she explained: "In the spirit world, I look like Halle Berry in the movie *X-Men*." Indeed, over there, her hair wasn't just silver, it was colored electric. Her face was more of a honey than ordinary caramel. Her eyes were two alluring moons. The garments draping her body reflected beams of fluorescent light.

Donna's interior wealth and sense of majesty explain the quiet dignity with which she carried herself in her apartment. In contrast to her simple appearance, being in Donna's presence on that first day felt like meeting a queen, a dignitary visiting from heaven, so to speak, except that her entourage of attendants were invisible. Yet to Donna, these presences were alive and real. They were not a figment of her imagination, nor did she assume they were part of a shared empirical reality available to ordinary human beings like me. Rather, for Donna, these ghosts inhabited a third area of experience *between* herself and the world, or what Donald Winnicott calls the "the *potential space* between . . . the individual and society."[17]

This third area of cultural experience is what Emilie Townes refers to as the "fantastic." As she writes:

> I argue that the fantastic is not limited to the worlds of literature but goes beyond to form a part of the cultural production of our realities—it is in the very fabric of the everyday. . . . The fantastic is the hesitation experienced by a person who knows only the laws of nature confronting an apparently supernatural event—it is defined in relation to the real and the imaginary. . . . Yet the fantastic is even more. It is also being comfortable with the supernatural or what may seem supernatural to others. In other words,

the fantastic may be the everyday for those who live in it. They
may not find the presence of ghosts or shifted realities unusual. . . .
Only those of us who sit outside these worlds must ponder what
they "see," "feel," "know" because our realities are challenged in
the face of the fantastic. . . . However, it is not only ghosts and
shifted realities that comprise the fantastic. It may also be structures of domination and subordination.[18]

Indeed, Donna's daily life was spent travailing in this fantastic realm between the real and the imaginary, and ghosts, both
sinister and friendly, occupied this figurative place. Donna often
experienced ghosts as the "the things behind the things," that
is, historical presences, misrecognized as such, that shape oppressive structures, institutions, and the minds and bodies of those
who habituate themselves within the everyday.[19] And she was
aware of friendly ghosts too, many of whom she collaborated
with to free people from their transgenerational traumas. The
extent to which the fantastic was embedded within the fabric of
Donna's everyday life became immediately clear to me when, as
soon as I entered her apartment, her body began to shake, her
eyes closed, her lips quivered, and, suddenly, she felt invisible
presences rush through her veins.

In an instant, the person standing before me became more.
From her mouth flowed a series of sounds incomprehensible to
me, which Donna called her "tongues," a divine language meant
to invoke the presence of the Holy Spirit and cleanse my aura of
evil. Donna offered me, her guest, the gift of healing, and, after
she spoke tongues and felt satisfied that both the room and my
thoughts were clear of unconscious distractions, she turned to
me with a smile.

"Your ancestors are talking to me, Onaje," she chuckled with
delight. "They love you so much, and they have so much to say

to you. Your ancestors standing around you right now. I'm lookin' right at 'em, some mean looking spirits." Donna rolled her eyes up to fix on an empty corner of the living room. "But I ain't scared of um. They ain't gonna punk me. I'm a child of God!" she exclaimed. "But they are mean looking. They have daggers as weapons and they are African. You are a warrior, Onaje. They want you to let go of that fear in your heart. You have a mission." Donna appeared to be translating the daggers and meanness of my ancestral spirits as a sign that I needed to be more steadfast and courageous in facing the challenges of my life head on. She was exercising her gifts of discernment.

"What?" Donna suddenly stopped to scold an ancestral ghost in midsentence. "What? Well, you brought him in here. If you got so much to say, then say it! Shoot, messing with me taking up my time," Donna scowled, annoyed at how demanding my African forebears were being at that moment. "Onaje, your ancestors are so excited they won't let me be! They want you to not be afraid. That's why I was sent here to talk to you," Donna confessed, acknowledging that our meeting was part of a larger plan. "Cause even though God has a plan for your life, you needed a little help to see it. I'm gonna lay hands on you today and after I lay hands on you, blessings, tons and tons of blessings gonna come your way."

Donna then explained further how our meeting fit into God's plan: "You see, this is gonna blow your mind, but we were very close in a previous life, but I wasn't the way I was supposed to be, and I steered you away from your true purpose the last time. But now I am the way God wants me to be, and we are meeting now so I can steer you in the right direction this time. I can make up for the wrong I did before." Donna leaned forward, looked at me intently, and said: "You won't believe me, but I was your mother in a previous life." My eyes widened, and she smiled. "I didn't say I was your wife now! Don't get it twisted," she laughed after seeing the look on my face. "I said I was your mother. You are my son!" Donna would later reveal that the ancestral spirits that protected her were African, too. We were part of the same tribe, so to speak, and so our meeting was naturally God's will, since African souls were known to reincarnate within the same family.

"It's not me, Onaje," Donna continued. "I can't take no credit for what comes through. I am a servant of God, and I ain't no mind reader. People's angels, they just talk to me and since your angels are always with you, they know you better than you know yourself." She began to chuckle. "God works in mysterious ways!" she exclaimed, shaking her head. "I ain't even gonna tell you, Onaje [what I just heard]. [But I will say] it's not just you and Jason that's on this path of basketball and healing. There is three of you. The three of y'all been on the same path and don't even know it. But I ain't gonna tell you who the third person is. Besides, God likes surprises, and I ain't gonna get in the way of God's pleasure. I want you to experience what God wants you to feel." Donna smiled, looking at me and Jason, and the single empty chair at the end of the wooden table.

"You see that empty chair?" she asked. "That empty chair symbolizes the absence of the third person I'm talking about. You see, this is the Holy Spirit's way of showing you one person is missing from this conversation. You see how spirit works with the things around you if you are willing to see?" Donna asked, attempting to illustrate to us how ordinary objects could be read as spiritual texts, and absences could signify presences. "Okay, I'll tell you," she relented. "The third person is your brother. He's going to help you and Jason. You're going to make films together." Donna made me smile. I loved my older brother, even though I hadn't seen him in a long time, and I had always hoped he and I might one day bond over our shared love of storytelling.

After Donna revealed the role my brother would play in my life, she rose up and walked toward me, her body trembling as a result of her close proximity to the spirit world. She placed her palms on my shoulders and began to pray. "Now, give me your hands," she said, grasping them. "Thank you, Holy Spirit. Yes, I feel your light all around me. Yes, give him your light. Use this boy's hands to write stories, Holy Spirit. I see books and books and books flying into your head, Onaje. Bless this your child. He is a tree, Father God, a tree of wisdom. I am made of light, but Onaje is a tree in your garden, Father God. Water him, Father God. Let his roots grow deep, and his branches grow wide and strong, Father God." As I closed my eyes, I heard the most melodious voice bellow from Donna's lips, the sound of which seemed to be opera. As this other-worldly voice filled the space, her living room began to empty of things that were attached to this world. It was as if we had entered a parallel dimension, one that somehow existed at the same time and within the same space as the dilapidated Housing Projects and violent streets of Roxbury.

Once the song ended, Donna shifted back to her normal self and almost immediately explained the source of the music. It came from the Hummingbird, she said, a spiritual being that inhabited her body whenever Donna was ready to seal her prayers. When the Hummingbird sang, thousands of angels materialized to listen to the sweetness of her voice, and their presence naturally cleared the space of residual evil, ensuring Donna's prayers would land on heavenly ears. Much like the vulture in the Yoruba Òrìsà religions of Africa and the Americas, Donna's Hummingbird proved to be a divine messenger.[20]

After listening to the Hummingbird, I was overwhelmed. Donna had skillfully labored in the realm of the fantastic to unburden my unconscious mind of self-limiting thoughts, with no expectation of anything in return. Her selfless gift of spiritual agency touched me deeply. And she was right: I was chronically stressed. The strain of being a young Black man from the streets of Roxbury, who left that world to find success in white academia in order to tell stories such as Donna's, was a constant source of doubt and fear.[21] But Donna was also right that I was a warrior, with enough ancestral memory to meet and exceed the challenges of my journey.

"Take some of this holy oil that I have blessed, Onaje," Donna offered, "and this charcoal, frankincense, and myrrh." She handed me the oils and incense as Jason and I prepared to leave. "When you leave here," she assured me, "your life will begin to change because of what we did today. Use the oil to rub the middle of your forehead and your body whenever you feel the need to cleanse your spirit. To cleanse your house, burn the frankincense and myrrh on the charcoal. Make sure you open up all your windows now and turn off your smoke detector. This stuff smokes up the whole house. Now, I know you live on campus [at the time I was teaching at Phillips Academy in Andover, Massachusetts, and supervising the dormitories], so make sure you turn off them smoke detectors, or else you'll wake up the whole building. This will help make your house holy."

As Donna handed me the bottle with its holy contents, I had a million questions. Why did she refer to me as a tree in her prayer? Could she have known that I had an affinity for sacred trees, so much so that I had traveled to Nigeria, in western Africa, to study them? Donna was obviously drawing from biblical imagery relating to the "tree of the knowledge of good and evil,"[22] but I had never heard a Christian refer to a *person* as a "tree of knowledge," or themselves as being "made of light," or of being possessed by spirit birds and ancestors that could move in and out of human bodies and speak to the living in real time. Such views of reality seemed more resonant with indigenous African and American Indian theologies than with the Abrahamic Christian faith of Donna's upbringing. Did she combine her Catholic and Baptist beliefs with the Afro-Jamaican traditions of her ancestral past? Was Donna's lived religion a collection of practices, similar to the African American folk religions of the American South that Zora Neale Hurston was known for chronicling, only in a contemporary, urban northern register?[23] As Jason and I made our way toward the door, Donna had one final message of encouragement for me.

"I had a vision," she pulled me aside, "where I saw the gate. The doors of heaven, the windows of heaven opened up, and I saw water with names in it being poured out the window. And the water was named. And they were telling me your name was in the water. And it was pouring. And all the names were written in black. And all I could just see was names. I don't know who these people were. It was like the water opened up. This was a waking vision. I simply closed my eyes, and I could just see it. And then I saw these names pouring out of the window, streams of water with people's names. I saw doors were closed that would be opened. I saw all this."

"Why were people's names in the water?" I asked.

"Blessings. Blessings. People with names," Donna responded. "God wanted me to let his children know that their prayers were being answered and that he has not forgotten about them."

I hugged Donna. "That's a beautiful vision. I'd like to come back again to learn more about your visions of life in Roxbury. Is that okay?"

"My spirit is feeling you," Donna said warmly. "Yes, that's okay."

And at those words, Jason and I turned and walked out of Donna's apartment, descended her building's steps, and entered the Roxbury night. I paused and took in the darkness. I couldn't believe I had been in the presence of a spiritual genius from my own neighborhood who inhabited an-other world. In that moment, I made a promise to myself: to return to Roxbury to listen to her story, for as long as it took.

I have organized this book into three sections. Part 1, "Daughter of Darkness," introduces Donna as a young girl, living in the Columbia Point Housing Projects of inner-city Boston. There, she painfully acknowledges, "the devil had his way with me." Keeping Urie Bronfenbrenner's ecological systems theory in mind, I explore the overlapping dimensions of violence (structural, institutional, interpersonal) that circumscribe Donna's life options.[24] Eventually we come to see how the triple evils of Black female oppression—racism, sexism, and poverty—haunt Donna throughout these years, driving her to an attempted suicide. In part 2, "Metamorphosis," Donna emerges from the darkness of her past after a harrowing encounter with the Holy Spirit and Jesus. As a result of her incarnation of the Holy Spirit, she becomes aware of "the things behind the things" and grasps for the fantastic. This section ends with the Holy Spirit revealing Donna's true name to her: "My child, you will be called Child of Light now." In part 3, "Child of Light," Donna receives her spiritual weapons from the Holy Spirit, who appoints her as warrior prophet for the disinherited and isolated members of American society. As an adept of spiritual warfare, she teleports throughout the universe to face the ghosts of American power that "can speak the language of your thoughts and desires . . . [and] can harm you without seeming ever to touch you."[25] In the final scene, the Holy Spirit permits Donna to enter an underworld that she refers to as hell, where she sees what hatred does to the souls of the dead. In those dark canyons, Donna prepares to "take back everything that the devil stole from me." At the end of the book, I also include a brief discussion on methodology.

I

DAUGHTER OF DARKNESS

1

"THE DEVIL HAD HIS
WAY WITH ME"

*So de white man throw down de load and tell de nigger man
tuh pick it up. He pick it up because he have to, but he don't tote
it. He hand it to his womenfolks. De nigger woman is de mule
uh de world so fur as Ah can see. Ah been prayin' fuh it tuh be different wid you. Lawd, Lawd, Lawd!*

—Zora Neale Hurston, *Their Eyes Were Watching God*

L ooks like there is fire," huffed the taxi driver, as he and
his passenger, Olivia, peered through the windshield at
the standstill traffic. In the distance they could see the

blue-and-white Boston Police vehicles flashing their strobe lights and hear the deafening sirens of the Boston Fire trucks.

"What?!" Olivia half-asked the driver, her mother's intuition kicking in. She pushed the car door open, left the baby formula she had just purchased on the backseat, and ran up the hill toward her apartment in Roxbury. Olivia was visiting her mother-in-law's home right off of Warren Street and MLK Boulevard with her husband, Noah, and their three baby girls, just a stone's throw away from the home of Ella Little Collins, where Malcolm X and his half-sister lived in the 1940s, two decades before.

Olivia could see the flames bursting through the apartment windows as she bolted up the hill. A crowd was gathering, and a friend of the family ran up to Olivia to deliver the devastating news.

"They were able to get Stella and Maya out, but they couldn't reach Donna." Olivia ignored the messenger, pushing passed him and running straight to the burning building. The firefighters and police officers blocked her as she tried to enter. Olivia let out a blood-curdling scream as she became tangled in their arms.

Unbeknownst to Olivia, little Donna was still alive inside. At that moment, she happened to be standing in her bedroom closet, paralyzed by fear, a bright, white, long-sleeved cashmere sweater between her small body and the flames. The room was hot, and thick black smoke poured in from the cracks above the closet door. Suddenly her closet door opened and a man stood in front of her, glowing, his face soft and gentle, unfazed by the flames raging around him. The man peered down at the little girl and spoke to her, but words did not come from his mouth. Donna did not see his lips move at all. Instead, she heard a voice, clear as day, in her mind. She felt him say, "Come out of the closest, don't be scared." The man reached out his open hand. Donna's little body trembled as she lifted her fingers to meet his. The man grasped her white sleeve gently, about five inches above her wrist.

"Go down to the floor," he told her, again through closed lips, slowly bending his knees to demonstrate just how the little girl should move. Donna knelt behind the glowing man but, for some reason, no longer felt afraid as she crawled out of the closet beneath the dark smoke. She followed the man for what felt like an eternity, until suddenly something large and heavy bumped against her. It was the big black boot of a fireman hitting the landing of the stairs that led out of the building. Surprised to have knocked into the little girl beneath the thickness of the smoke, the fireman reached down and gripped Donna's body tight as she took in his mask, his Darth Vader breath, his bright yellow jacket, and the large oxygen tank strapped across his back. The sound of his heavy breathing was what scared Donna the most, but she surrendered in his arms as he carried her down the stairs and out of the inferno. Donna looked back, but the man with the glowing hands who made his thoughts hers had disappeared.

Olivia couldn't believe her eyes. There she was, her precious daughter, suspended in the fireman's arms, alive, though her body was covered in thick layers of black soot. Donna's hairline had been scorched with second-degree burns. The skin on her hands had partly melted away, giving them the look of an old woman for the rest of her life. The toxic, black-gray smoke collapsed both her lungs, precipitating lifelong struggles with severe asthma, and underneath all the layers of smoke and soot, there was a mystery that neither the doctors nor Olivia could understand.

"She has an oval-shaped burn mark underneath her sweater," they told Olivia at the hospital. "It doesn't look like a normal burn mark. It's about five inches above her wrist, and the sweater covering it remains unburned. Do you think she put on the sweater during the fire?" the doctor wondered.

"No, I don't think so," Olivia responded.

"In all that smoke, I don't believe so, either," said the doctor. "It is a miracle she even survived."

It had been five years since Donna had been claimed by the fire, and for the most part she had forgotten the incident altogether, especially her encounter with the glowing man who introduced her to the supernatural power within the flames. All that remained was the unconscious terror that gripped Donna whenever the sound of fire engine sirens tore through her neighborhood. Once a massive red fire truck, its lights flashing, sirens blaring, sped down the street in her direction, triggering Donna's undiagnosed PTSD. Donna bolted straight toward the truck, "like something was pushing me to do it." Witnesses gasped as she hurled her body at the red machine, before the truck swerved, missing the middle schooler by inches. A neighbor collected the hyperventilating girl.

"Why did you that?" he asked.

"I don't know why. I don't know why," Donna cried.

Donna didn't fully understand it, but she ran whenever she heard fire trucks approaching. On another occasion, when Donna's neighbor's back porch caught on fire, her mother screamed, "Everyone get out of the house!" As soon as Donna heard the sirens in the distance, she hopped down a flight of steps, clean through the front door, and ran straight in front of the red ladder truck coming her way.

"My mother's friend snatched me in the nick of time. I would have been run over," Donna shook her head. And to make matters more complicated, Olivia and her husband, Noah, had just decided to move the family to one of Boston's poorest and most isolated African American subsidized housing communities, the Columbia Point Housing Projects.

The Point was a low-income housing complex built on a dumpsite, located on a narrow peninsula that pointed toward the cool New England waters of Dorchester Bay. The spot was a landing point for white Puritan settlers in the seventeenth century. In 1968, however, it had become the site of the largest government housing development in all New England, where several thousand black and brown bodies were crammed into more than 1,500 low-income apartments stacked on top of one another like sardine cans.

Of course, even before it was built, the Boston Housing Authority was aware that the Point would be a space of social abandonment, isolation, and exile from the rest of the city and completely ignored the dire warnings in the planning board's report to the Boston City Council:

> Boston has a serious responsibility toward these people to assure that they will have not only "decent, safe, and sanitary" dwellings, but a decent, safe, and sanitary environment as well, as far as possible. It must be remembered that these people will reside on a peninsula with water on three sides and a heavily traveled arterial highway on the fourth. Moreover, their isolation will be further accentuated by the fact that for a considerable distance the opposite side of that highway is unpopulated. Thus, many of the facilities and amenities essential to good community living must be provided within Calf Pasture [Columbia Point] itself, or not at all.[1]

Yet when Boston's Mayor Hynes opened the housing project to residents, notes researcher Jane Roessner, trash "dumps were still in operation twenty-four hours a day, right next door to Columbia Point. There was no public transportation, no school, no grocery store, no church."[2]

Roessner writes further: "The story of Columbia Point in the late 1960s and 1970s is a depressing one: a once-proud community disintegrating, torn by racial strife, drugs, crime, and neglect. An increasingly fearful community, where people retreat behind locked doors. Finally, a hopeless community abandoned, defensive, and ultimately self-destructive. The project's decline is a story filled with frustration and failure that no one is eager or proud to tell."[3]

It was within this context of "social death" and structural inequality born out in the streets of Boston that Olivia seemed to become angrier and angrier each time the sirens caused her little girl to behave erratically.[4]

Of course, it didn't help that Donna's mother had mental health issues of her own. Olivia loved her children, but she was an abusive parent who had bipolar disorder and bouts of clinical depression. She often fell into an especially foul mood while driving Donna to her weekly psychiatrist appointments to treat her fear of fire trucks. On those treacherous trips to the doctor's office, she'd turn around and yell "you're so stupid!" or "you bitch!" at her little girl. Olivia shouted so many obscenities at Donna that once they arrived at the doctor's office, she made Donna promise not to tell the doctor what had happened. "Don't tell him anything about my personal business!" she warned Donna, as they approached the door of the kind, middle-aged white doctor.

At first Donna viewed these visits as a form of punishment for being a "stupid bitch," and she didn't want to get her mother into trouble, so she barely spoke, especially when the doctor asked about her life in the Point. She didn't dare share how her mother chased her around the apartment with a knife and sometimes beat her for no apparent reason or repeatedly called her a bitch. She just sat there, periodically rubbing her right arm above the wrist, which she did out of habit, at times because the oval-shaped crescent itched like a day-old mosquito bite.

"What's on your arm?" the psychiatrist finally asked Donna. "Can you show me your arm?" Donna obliged and showed the doctor the strange burn on her skin that looked like a full moon.

"I was burned," she told him.

"Yes, your mom says you were trapped in a house fire. It's a miracle that you survived," the doctor responded, as Donna suddenly realized, for the first time, that the blaze was the reason Olivia brought her daughter to see the psychiatrist—not to get the bitch out of her. "Do you sometimes still feel afraid of the fire?" the doctor asked.

"Yes," Donna nodded. She was terrified of fire and especially the sound of fire trucks or the sight of firefighters. She thought of the fireman in the oxygen mask who had rescued her, the sound of his heavy breath, and it sent chills up her spine.

"Donna, I know it seems strange to say this, but I want you to know that the very thing that you are afraid of, saved your life," the psychiatrist said, giving Donna a moment to ponder his words. Donna had never thought of the fire like that before, and not until she became grown would she come to see her near-death experience as a spiritual summons—a baptism by fire, so to speak—calling her to fulfill a special destiny encoded in the transformational power of the flames.[5]

"In the physical world," Donna would later explain, "we are trained to fear fire. But in the spirit realm, fire is the purifying light of God. The enemy tried to make me afraid and abuse the very thing that was the source of my power." Indeed, for Donna, the enemy or the devil was her figurative way of naming the various forms of structural evil in her life. They could "harm you without seeming to ever touch you,"[6] by configuring sites of racial, economic, and gender-based violence that fanned flames of terror in Columbia Point Housing Projects.

"BURN, BABY, BURN"

"The devil had his way with me," an exasperated Donna admitted about her teenage years in the Point. Yellow police tape zigzagged across several vacant apartment doorways and stairwells in the hot brick high-rise buildings that made up the housing project. The apartments were empty because their prior occupants had been arrested in a drug enforcement raid and sent to prison. The darkened hallways smelled like urine and sometimes feces. The elevators were broken, and on sidewalks, used needles and syringes lay for curious children to fondle. Some neighborhood teenagers had torn down the yellow tape, snuck into the vacant apartments, loosely decorated the interior, and claimed the spaces as "pads." Landing a vacant became so routine that when a friend found an apartment that fit her tastes, she would have the neighborhood kids over for a housewarming of sorts—Projects-style. Young boys and girls, each no more than sixteen years old, could be seen walking around a friend's vacant, complimenting the new occupant: "I really like what you did here." "Girl, you got two bedrooms!" "Wow, look at that view!"

After visiting several of her friends' pads, Donna pulled her girlfriend, Sarah, aside and asked if she wanted to become roommates in a vacant of their own. Sarah nodded with enthusiasm, and the two sixteen-year-olds agreed to meet at night on the rooftop of a high-rise to go apartment hunting. Each building in the housing projects was connected to the next one by a large platform. If you wanted to do anything illicit without being noticed, especially by the police, the best way was to climb up to the rooftop of one building, cross over to the next one, and then the next, before descending several flights and walking out the front door of a building far away from your original location. Donna and Sarah planned to make use of this well-worn piece of street knowledge to check out as many vacant apartments as possible.

The girls walked off the roof and down the stairwell to make their way to the first vacant on their mental list. Moving aside the yellow police tape barring the doorway, they entered the apartment and checked to see if the layout fit their tastes and needs. Donna wanted a large bedroom with a window, and they both wanted a spacious living area and nice kitchen.

Once they found a suitable apartment, the two girls planned its interior design, combining their allowances to shop after school for cool African American–themed posters at Roxbury's Nubian Notions and subtle lighting and sultry curtains to neatly drape over their windows-with-a-view. Next on their list was proper furniture, although the girls did not have enough money to purchase a dining table set, couches, or beds and have them delivered.

Instead, one of the girls remembered some really nice pieces they had seen earlier in a different vacant, so one night, at one o'clock in the morning, they carried a kitchen table and four wooden chairs that matched their developing sense of décor out of one vacant apartment and into their new, humble abode. If you had been watching the streets of the Columbia Point Housing Projects one cool, summer evening in the 1970s, you might have seen these two shadowy figures with tables and chairs on their heads, hurrying between the buildings, before disappearing through a series of doorways to set up their new home with glee.

Once their apartment was settled, it became Donna and Sarah's go-to afterschool destination. They would run up several flights of stairs past other apartments occupied by rent-paying residents, swing their door open, and throw their bags down before relaxing on the couch or deciding what to cook for dinner (spaghetti and meatballs was their first meal). But there was one problem. The door to the apartment was missing a lock, which meant anyone in the Projects searching for a vacant could waltz in at night after crossing the rooftop, as they had done. What the two girls needed was the Projects' version of a handyman. So one evening Donna went to see a couple of Puerto Rican guys in the neighborhood, stereotypically perceived as lock pickers in the Point.

"Back then, at the Point, the Puerto Ricans were known for picking locks to get into cars and apartments, so we asked one. God rest his soul, he's not living now. He taught us how to put a lock on the door and put a key in it," explained Donna. Although the lock was fragile, it worked—and their locksmith even fashioned a key that turned the doorknob, which made the girls feel a bit more secure in their new place.

"We're just coming and going like it's our apartment," Donna said, shaking her head in embarrassment.

In many ways, Donna's vacant apartment was her first refuge from the daily drama of life in the Point, especially for a young girl who was beginning to feel the unwanted sexual attention of boys and men in the neighborhood. Even at sixteen years old, Donna knew that boys and grown men were drawn to her large breasts, round buttocks, and womanly figure and were always trying to "get some." Clearly, her body had been subsumed under the prevailing narrative in the neighborhood about Black women and girls—that they were inherently promiscuous and "always want the D."[7] Nevertheless, Donna's apartment felt like her own safe haven from those oppressive assumptions, where she could buffer the effects of her mother's "Bitch" label and counter the myths of Black female hypersexuality.

Donna had consensual sex for the first time a couple of years earlier with a boy her age named Garcia. He was a cute Latino boy with muscles and soft wavy hair, and Donna was attracted to his nice smile. The two climbed several flights of stairs to the rooftop of one of the Project buildings where they stripped off their clothes excitedly, kissed, and made love. Then Garcia stood up quickly and asked Donna to wait for a few minutes until he returned. Donna was confused, but rather than wait in silence she decided to pick her blouse off the gravel rooftop and slip it on. She then reached for her panties, just as Garcia remerged from the stairwell with a male friend.

"I told you! I told you I just hit that!" Garcia bragged. The two boys pointed and laughed at Donna hysterically as they watched her attempt to put her panties on, the shame of having her body exhibited and displayed "in a museum of otherness" clearly visible on her young face.[8] After reducing her to a sexual object, the boys slapped each other's hands and disappeared, leaving Donna to pick up the pieces of her fractured flesh in tears.

"THE FIRST TIME SOMEONE TRIED TO RAPE ME"

Donna's vacant apartment was the only place in the Projects where her body hadn't been reduced to a thing by the pornotropic gaze of others. As a young woman she had been automatically excluded from performing her identity in male-centered spaces in the Point, such as the street corner or the playing field, which was part of the reason why Donna and Sarah sought out a vacant apartment—to find a place where they could feel fully human on their own. Though the intersection of gender, race, and poverty had pushed Donna into this culturally assigned place, she was determined to turn her apartment into an early site of Black girl resistance. The door to her world was protected by a faux lock, but at least she could exercise a fragile sense of control over who she let in or chose to exclude from her private life.

Donna revealed, as we sat in her living room, that her sense of security came crashing down "the first time that someone tried to rape me. I fought him off of me, though," she seethed. "He didn't get that either." The day of the attack, Donna had taken a chance with the seventh-floor elevator outside of Sarah's mother's apartment. The mere act of entering and exiting low-income housing project buildings was a dangerous activity for girls and women in the Point, navigating narrow staircases in the dark, riding piss-soaked elevator cars up and down multiple floors. The fact that they possessed female body parts put riders in constant danger. Nevertheless, Donna chose to risk the elevator that day, stepping into the car and pressing the button for the ground floor, hoping the doors would close before anyone else entered. Donna waited anxiously as the car dropped, the "bing" of the bell sounding out each floor. She felt a moment of relief as the car hit its destination, but, as the doors opened, she saw that the long corridor leading to the building's exit was unlit. The hall was eerily silent. "I said, well, maybe I could just dash to the door and just go out," but as soon as Donna left the elevator, a large male figure stepped up behind her and stuck something sharp into her side.

Two men dragged Donna back into the elevator, forced a piece of cloth around her face, and closed the doors behind them. Donna stood there, knife to her back and blindfolded, the "bing" of the elevator car now inspiring terror as it rose successive floors.

"Get off the elevator and watch your step," one of the men commanded. Donna stepped off the elevator and was pushed down a long hallway until she heard one of the men stick a key in a door. Once inside, they closed the door behind them and removed her blindfold. "I looked at 'em, and I was like, are you crazy? My mother will kill you. I knew who they were," Donna remembered, which aligns with research that shows most survivors of sexual assault know their attackers.[9] "They were like, 'Oh, you're gonna give it up tonight!'"

Apparently Donna was known by men in the Projects for acting like her sexuality belonged to her alone. This angered her two acquaintances, who couldn't fathom the idea that the sexual labor of an African American girl living in their neighborhood wasn't theirs for the taking. "You walk around the Projects acting like you're all that," they said. "You too good to give it up to anybody?" one sneered, as Donna was dragged to a mattress in an otherwise empty bedroom. Donna resisted. One of the rapists picked her up and slammed her down onto the mattress. The other jumped on top of her, snatched off her pants and panties, and busted her shirt wide open, commanding the other to pry Donna's legs open.

"And I'm fighting. I mean, I will not stop fighting. The guy's punching me in my face, boom, boom, and I'm still fighting. I keep fighting. So then I played it off, and said 'okay, okay, come on.' But once he got close with his penis, I grabbed it and tried to break it! He gets up with his penis in my hand and he says to his friend, 'She got me, she got me!' His friend then tried to put his penis inside me, and I tried to break his, too. And he's like, 'She got me too!' They both run into the corner, licking their wounds. And I'm sitting there, saying, 'You know what, you are not gonna touch me. You're not gonna come inside me. I'd rather die first!'"

Donna wasn't bluffing. She would rather take her own life than allow a man to violate her humanity. While her two attackers writhed in pain, Donna made her way over to a large window overlooking the street and climbed out. Perched on the window ledge, her legs dangling several stories above the ground, the men screamed, "Don't jump! You're on the seventh floor!"

"If you come near me, I'll jump out this window. I'd rather die," Donna threw back at them, but then she saw a third man enter the room, which scared her even more, and she inched even further out of the window.

"I don't want a murder rap," one of the men repeated again and again. "We promise not to touch you. You're not the first girl we've brought up here. We've got several girls up here to have sex with us. Why can't you just do it, and we'll let you go?" one rapist asked.

"Because my mother told me not to have sex. All of you know my mother," replied Donna. "I'll jump."

After several minutes, in full view of the street and wearing only a shirt and no panties, Donna climbed back into the apartment. The men gave her a jacket and promised not to hurt her. "Why didn't you just give it up?" they asked again. "We've had so many girls up here."

"Because I have respect for myself," Donna replied, before walking out the front door.

Though it was decades later, Donna broke down in tears as she sat on her living room couch and shared her story with me.

"It was like I was always fighting the person they saw me as on the outside," she sobbed. "They made me feel nasty and disgusting. I could not love myself for who I was when they made me feel dirty and filthy. I couldn't embrace my breasts, embrace my hips, embrace my body. I couldn't look in the mirror and embrace myself, because they kept seeing me as nasty. They said they had sex with all these older girls that I looked up to. But I didn't want to disappoint my mother. She raised me to be a strong woman and to fight, and I'd rather die." After leaving the apartment, Donna walked straight to her mother's house, drew a warm bath, and locked the bathroom door. "I sat in the bath, and I literally tried to claw my skin off. I hated my body. I hit it and punched it and yelled at it. No one in the apartment heard me cry. When I was in there long, my mother asked me what was wrong. I just said, 'Nothing, I'm tired.'" Donna's body was no longer her own.

As time wore on, Donna came to realize that her traumatic experience of sexual assault was a common occurrence among many Black girls and women in the Point and other housing projects in Boston and the United States. As researchers have noted, race, gender, and poverty intersect in troubling ways so that "African American women who live in low-income housing complexes or are homeless most often are in communities with high rates of violence and substance use and abuse that ultimately increases their vulnerability to being sexually assaulted."[10] Moreover, given that "there was a time in U.S. history in which rape laws were race specific and did not recognize African American women as victims," and that we continue to live in an American culture in which "oppressive and stereotypical images support the racist belief system that African American women are unrapeable," it is understandable that Donna didn't even consider reporting her sexual assault to the police or members of her own family after it happened. Instead, she kept the pain and rage to herself, suspecting others might even accuse her of being promiscuous.

Once she was sexually assaulted, Donna no longer felt safe in the vacant apartment she shared with Jackie. Her feeling of being unprotected intensified when, one afternoon, Donna put her key in the makeshift lock only to have someone on the other side yank the door open. It was Garcia, the boy from the rooftop.

"What are you doing here?" Donna asked as Garcia stood, butt naked, in her living room. The sight of his body desecrating her private space infuriated Donna as she blew past him toward her bedroom, slamming the door behind her.

"I just had sex with Sarah," Garcia bragged, reminding Donna of the day he had humiliated her on the rooftop. "And now you're next," he chuckled.

"Get out!" Donna shouted, coming back into the living room. "Sarah, how could you let him in here?" she screamed. All the resentment from years before came rushing back, as Donna stormed through the apartment, throwing objects at the walls, knocking over chairs, demanding at the top of her lungs that Garcia leave. It was as if Garcia being in her apartment, naked and uninvited, assaulted her all over again. When Garcia saw the rage in Donna's eyes, he quickly grabbed his clothes and ran out of the apartment, while Donna turned to Sarah and declared: "I'm burning it down. I'm burning this apartment to the ground." Donna grabbed a knife and some matches from the kitchen. Afraid, Sarah bolted from the apartment, leaving Donna with her blood boiling.

Donna stomped over to her bedroom and stared at the mattress, now a symbol of how dirty she felt about herself and sex in general. Part of her believed it was her fault. Maybe, if she didn't possess a womanly body, men wouldn't be so attracted to her. "Ain't no one laying up in here again. He ain't coming up in here," she screamed. She then took the knife and thrust it into the mattress over and over again, "as if I was stabbing Garcia," until the yellow foam burst from its belly, spilling out onto the bedroom floor. Dropping the knife, Donna tore a match from the pack and struck a flame, placing it directly onto the foam, until the foamy flesh set ablaze. "This was my way of releasing all of the dirtiness that happened to me in the Projects," she explained.

As smoke filled her vacant, Donna ran down several flights of steps to the sidewalk to observe the inferno. "That's so sad," she exclaimed to the police officers and firefighters who had arrived at the site. When an officer asked her if she saw who set the fire, Donna shook her head, "No, it's just so sad." And because of the gendered assumptions of the police department, Donna wasn't the least bit nervous about getting caught as she stood on the sidewalk, staring at the spectacle of smoke pouring out of the building. "I knew that they would never suspect a woman of setting the fire," Donna quipped. "They automatically assumed it had to be a man."

Donna's sister, Maya, stood at a distance, staring at Donna, knowing full well she had been responsible for the sea of flames. "I know you did it," Maya declared as Donna approached her. "I know that was your apartment, and I know you've been setting abandoned cars on fire, too!"

Donna bowed her head, acknowledging she had become the neighborhood arsonist. Given that she had almost died in a fire more than a decade earlier, it was ironic that she had come to abuse the element to cope with her emotional and physical pain. "Be quiet, Maya. You don't know anything."

"I'm going to tell Mommy," warned Maya.

"Okay, what do you want?" Donna bargained.

"Do my chores. You have to do the dishes for a week!"

"Okay, fine," Donna agreed. "Now leave me alone." The following week Donna found herself at the kitchen sink in her mother's apartment scrubbing dishes each night "rather doing that then get a lashing from my mother." Donna's safe haven in the Projects had been incinerated, and after she and Sarah reconciled, they had to find a new place to call home.

SEARCHING FOR A NEW VACANT

"Listen, I don't like going in these apartments at night," Donna whispered, as she and Sarah moved through the rooms and across rooftops of the high-rises, searching for a new home. Finally they spotted an apartment that looked empty enough, and Sarah approached, trying to twist the doorknob. It seemed locked. Donna suggested they turn around and leave, since someone might be living inside. "Sarah, come on. Let's go!" she begged, but Sarah kept insisting, putting all her weight into the twist before the door finally cracked open just enough for her to peek inside.

"And then all of a sudden, she starts laughing. I'm like, 'What?' And she's just laughing. So I stand, get on my toes and I reach over her. This man's standing there, butt naked, and a woman is lying on the floor mattress. He's like, 'What you looking at?' Sarah's standing there laughing. I'm like, 'Sarah, come on, let's go!'" Donna and Sarah turned around and flew down the stairs, the two girls running as hard as they could to escape the building and what they witnessed.

As hard as they ran, though, Donna still heard footsteps chasing them, which seemed to be getting closer. So when she reached the last flight of steps leading to the building's exit, she jumped the whole staircase to land flat on the concrete outside.

"My backside was killing me. My buttocks hurt for days. Oh my God, I couldn't sit down," Donna remembered, grabbing her hip as we spoke in her apartment. When Donna looked up from the concrete to see who was behind her, her neighbor's face struck a bewildered expression.

"Donna, are you okay? Why are you running?"

Donna just shook her head. "Oh, it's nothing," she said, as she limped off the sidewalk with Sarah, hunched over in embarrassment. She was done with vacant apartments. If she could set them all on fire to protect women and girls in the neighborhood, she would.

Donna was not proud of being an arsonist, nor of stealing vacant apartments, nor of her sexual experiences in the Point. In fact, like most girls her age, she blamed herself for the pain she endured. And what she knew of religion only made matters worse. Her mother, Olivia, was a practicing Catholic, and as Donna learned during Sunday Mass, God loved holy women who didn't lie or steal and remained virgins until marriage. Donna even told her mother that she wanted to become a nun when she grew up, that she loved the beautiful tunics and modest veils they wore on their holy bodies during liturgical services. Now, as a girl who had had sex and burned things she hated, Donna felt unqualified to be in God's presence.

"I'm not proud of what I did. Now keep in mind, when I was doing this, I didn't have a daughter then. I was young and dumb. But you want to know something? I used to tell my mother I was gonna be a nun one day. My mom's religion at the time was Catholic and I always liked the nuns, especially what they would wear. And then after a while, I didn't think I was good enough to be a nun."

DONNA'S MOTHER

Donna received her initial conception of God and womanhood and her strong personality from her mother. Olivia did her best to attend Mass every Sunday, but when she couldn't, she prayed to Jesus and the Saints at her home altar, surrounded by family pictures, burning candles of the Saints, and a figure of Jesus in flowing white garb.

Olivia was also a community activist during the racial tumult of the 1960s in the lead-up to the Boston busing crisis of the 1970s.[11] Olivia stood on the front lines fighting drug addiction, anti-Black racism, sexual violence, and police brutality at the Point. Crack cocaine had already flooded the neighborhood, and it was common to find used syringes and needles strewn along the sidewalks in front of Donna's high-rise. Olivia would sometimes confront users shooting up outside of her apartment, at times angrily, risking her own life. One day an older man using drugs thrust his nose right in Olivia's face.

"You need to mind your business!" he shouted.

"He thought my mom was gonna back up," remembered Donna. "She didn't even flinch. But four days later, he tried to kill us with fire."

The day the opioid addict attempted to kill Donna's family with a firebomb, Donna was relaxing on the living room couch while her sister, Stella, who was now eight months pregnant, propped her feet up on the lounge chair. Feeling tired, Stella rose to go "lie down in the bedroom. All of a sudden, she comes out screaming and hollering, running out of the house, and I can't get nothing out of her but 'Fire!'"

Confused but no longer afraid of the flames, given that she was an arsonist herself, Donna ran back toward Stella's room, only to see Stella's bed engulfed in a blaze. The drug addict had

climbed several flights of stairs onto the roof of Donna's building, then had a friend swing his body over the roof's edge to
throw a Molotov cocktail through Stella's window. If he had
thrown the firebomb through an adjacent window, it would have
hit Stella directly.

"Who would do that to a person?" the police asked Olivia
after the fire had been extinguished. "My mother was in her
room, and all of a sudden, she just went to the window and looked
across the yard. She said, 'I know who did it.' She just knew. She
knew who it was. She knew. My mother had a lot of incidents
where this guy tried to harm her."

Olivia's community activism also made her a favorite target
of the white police officers who were determined to terrorize the
black and brown residents of the Point. One afternoon, Olivia
was nearly murdered by a policeman as she tried to stop two older
boys from beating up Stella. The boys had been chasing her down
the street, and when they caught her, they started throwing
punches and tried to kick Stella's pregnant stomach. But Stella
fought back hard. When Donna ran to the kitchen window to
see what was going on, she saw Stella "tearing them boys up.
She's beating both of them. She's got one in a headlock. She put
the other boy's head between a pair of steel bars." Donna smiled.
"She didn't need no help, not even from me."

But when their other sister, Maya, saw Stella getting jumped
by the two boys, she bolted out of the apartment, flew down the
stairs, and ran outside to the sidewalk to take up for her sister.

"Stella's down there. They're jumping on her!" someone ran
to tell Olivia, as she was cutting salt pork at the kitchen table.
Olivia jumped up from the greasy meat and ran downstairs,
unmindful of the kitchen knife, which she still held in her hands.
Just then, a patrol car came screaming around the block, driven
by an officer who "was known in our neighborhood as a racist.

Everyone in the Projects complained about this man, how he was just beating people up for no reason, stopping them, doing crazy stuff, and he never liked my mother. He never believed that the community could work with the police like she was trying to organize. He was totally against it. If you ask me," remarked Donna, "he acted like a member of the Ku Klux Klan."

"Give me the knife," the white patrol officer commanded Olivia, who suddenly realized the long kitchen blade was still in her hand.

"I'm gonna put the knife back in the house," Olivia assured the officer, as Donna ran behind her mother and gently took the knife out of her hand before running it back upstairs to the apartment. Hoping to avoid a confrontation, Olivia slowly turned around and started to follow Donna into the building and up the stairs—but the cop followed.

"We get right to the door, and this man literally pushes his way through our door, takes me and throws me to the left, throws my mother to the right, pulls his gun out, points it right at my mom's temple. The whole hallway's full of people screaming and yelling telling this man to put his gun away. My mother could see death coming. His partner is pleading with him not to shoot my mother, pleading with him." Refusing to back down, the white officer stepped toward Olivia and pulled the trigger, just as one of Olivia's neighbors jumped over the staircase banister and smacked the gun upward, directing the bullet to hit the ceiling.

"My mother was—thank you, Holy Spirit." Donna stopped in midsentence as she recalled the incident, to acknowledge being stirred by the presence of the Holy Spirit as she spoke. "My mother was literally in a traumatized state for two weeks. We had to have a homecare provider for two weeks because all she kept seeing was me thrown to the floor. She kept waking up out of her sleep calling my name, 'Donna!' When I'd come home from school, I would have to sit beside her on the couch. She wouldn't sleep in her bed anymore. 'Donna!' and they would say, 'Your mother's asking for you. She kept saying, 'Donna!' 'I'm right here, Mommy. I'm okay. I'm alright.'" Donna's voice cracked.

The continuous traumatization of the community and chronic police violence in the Projects probably contributed to Olivia's abusive behavior toward her own children. And tragically, Donna's experience of child abuse led her to believe she was unloved. "Sometimes we would physically fight, and I often felt like my mom didn't understand me. All my life, I felt like no one understood me, no one loved me. I felt like my mom didn't love me. If you love me, why were you always hitting me when I did something wrong? She put down the law, and I had to respect that, but she took a lot of her anger out on me. The way Tyler Perry represents Madea, that's my mama. Do you hear me? She might not have a 9mm Glock, but she laid the law. My mother's mother, God rest her soul, Nana Audree, was Jamaican. She was imported from Jamaica and the highest thing Jamaican people value is respect. It's respect of your mother and your father. So, every time we got into it, it was a sign of disrespect. One time my mother beat me up so bad I had to stay at my sister's house, and I could have left but I wanted my mom's love. My mom's love meant more to me than her beating me." Donna cried as she spoke of the intergenerational transmission of trauma in her family.[12]

On one such occasion, Donna's mother beat her so badly Donna didn't recognize herself in the mirror. When the police arrived, an officer pulled Donna into the bathroom and said,

"Listen, we can plainly see who the aggressor was in here. You just say the word right now and we'll take her to jail." But Donna wasn't capable of sending her own mother to prison.

"What do you want to do?" asked the policeman.

"Nothing," Donna replied, with a sense of resignation.

After the officer left the apartment, Donna looked at her face in the mirror. She was horrified. There were claw marks and scratches everywhere, as if one of the rabid rats that lived in the former city dump site that was Columbia Point had gnawed her face while she slept.[13] Olivia had taken a metal hookah she used for smoking weed and swung it across Donna's upper lip, leaving a huge gash. She then slammed Donna's young body up against the freezer, clawing her fingernails across her daughter's neck before trying to choke her out, well aware of Donna's history of severe asthma. Once Donna managed to get away, Olivia snatched her daughter from behind and threw her up against the cabinet, where Donna fell to the floor, a kitchen drawer containing knives popping open just above her head. Donna snatched a knife out of the drawer, which forced her mother to pull back, turn, and bolt out of the house before running down the street to Donna's aunt.

A few minutes later Olivia came storming back with Donna's aunt in tow, whom she had convinced that Donna had been the aggressor. "Donna, why are you doing this?" Olivia pleaded as she tried to push open their apartment door.

Each time Olivia made headway through the door, Donna jabbed the knife in the crevice to push her mother back. "No, you ain't coming up in here doing crazy on me like you did," Donna screamed.

Eventually Donna found a way to escape the apartment, running to her older sister's place before Olivia could figure out where she was. When Donna woke up the next morning, she saw her battered face clearly in the bathroom mirror. "Oh, my God. My face. I could not come out of my sister's house for three days. I was unrecognizable. I didn't know my face was like that until my nephew, Timothy, said, 'Auntie, what's wrong with your face?' And my brother-in-law, big James, he said: 'Donna, you need to go in the bathroom. You really need to go in the bathroom.' I saw my face. I had two black eyes. I was like, 'I've got to get out of here. If I don't get out of here, my mother's gonna kill me.'"

TEENAGE PREGNANCY

Feeling unwanted by her mother, Donna turned to the thought of having a baby of her own. "I thought, if I have a child, the child will love me for who I am. This child's not gonna judge me. I'm gonna be the world to this child. And at the time, everybody was getting pregnant, so I got pregnant with my oldest daughter," she explained, mirroring research that indicates that poverty, violence, and neglect at home and school are among the factors that place girls at risk of early teenage pregnancy.[14]

Donna carried Alexis in her womb for four months before the excitement of being pregnant began to fade into the reality of having to take care of another human being. "What did I get myself into?" Donna thought. "You're eighteen. You got no job, no money. You don't got nothing. I was so depressed," she explained, revealing her foreshortened sense of the future and declining mental health. "In findings from a sample of low-income abused African American women, Kaslow, Thompson, Brooks, and Twomey (2000) found that risk factors for attempting suicide were more severe negative life events, history of child maltreatment, high psychological distress and depression, hopelessness about the future, and alcohol and drug problems."[15]

So one evening after midnight, Donna walked out of her mother's apartment and made her way in the pouring rain to the ledge overlooking Dorchester Bay. As she gazed down, feelings of inadequacy and powerlessness became overwhelming, and she decided to end her life by jumping into the water. In that moment, though, two beams of light flashed in the darkness that startled her. When Donna turned around to see where the lights were coming from, she saw a security guard's patrol car stopped a short distance behind her. Getting out of his car, the young security guard approached Donna. He could see she had been crying, her tears mixed with raindrops on her caramel cheeks. Quietly and gently he spoke to the teenager, assuring her everything was going to be okay and asking if he could give her a ride home. There was something about his gentle voice that coaxed Donna away from the water's edge, and she agreed to sit in his patrol car, although she remained quiet the whole ride home. Little did the young officer realize he had saved two lives that evening.

Once Donna reached her mother's apartment, she pushed the front door open and walked past Olivia and her guests, who were smoking weed and listening to "Let's Get it On," by Marvin Gaye.[16] Surprisingly, Olivia followed her into the bedroom with a sincere look of concern. "Donna, everything's gonna be alright. I'm gonna help you. Everything's gonna be okay," she comforted her baby girl. Donna sobbed as she listened to Olivia. It was the first time she felt like her mother truly understood her, which was all she wanted. Donna curled up into a ball and fell asleep. When she woke a few minutes later, she was alone, staring at the ceiling above her bed, loathing her inability to control her fate. Then it happened for the first time. Donna felt her baby move inside her womb. "As soon as I felt that I was like, 'Wow!' I didn't know if I was having a boy or a girl, but for some reason, I said, 'Wow, she's moving!' I felt her go from my right side to the left side of my stomach. And from that moment on, my love was there for my daughter. My love was there. Having Alexis definitely changed my life because before she was born, I wanted to kill myself."

LEAVING HOME

When Alexis entered the world, Donna knew it would soon be time for her to leave home. "I would go back into a shelter first," she declared, rather than subject her daughter to the same abuse Donna had experienced growing up.

The day Donna decided to pack her bags, she found Olivia banging her fist against her sister Stella's bedroom door, while wielding a large kitchen knife in her other hand. "I go upstairs to say, 'Mom, stop. What are you doing?'" said Donna. "And she comes after me with the knife. That's the bipolar in my mother."

Donna ran upstairs to her bedroom, slamming the door behind her and placing her back against the wall. "She really tried to get at me. Then the phone rang. It was the housing management company I had been working with to get a new apartment. I said my mother has a knife, and she's trying to kill me. The whole time, my mother is jabbing the door with the knife. They could hear my mother hollering and screaming in the background talking about 'I'm gonna kill you.' So, the woman on the phone says to me, 'Does your mother have a doctor?' and I said, 'Yeah.' 'You go to your doctor. You get a letter from them describing the altercation with your mother, her status and everything, and you'll get that apartment.' Then the woman called the police and when the police arrived, my mom switched it off so fast. The police knocked on the door. I looked out the window. They've got their guns pointed at my mother. I opened my window and said, 'Officer, I'm here,' and they came in." Olivia eventually talked the officers out of arresting her, but they warned, "If we come back here again, we're taking you to jail."

Donna couldn't stay any longer, not if she wanted to hold on to any love for her mother. "I wanted to leave the house physically intact, and I didn't want to leave hating my mother, and I *was* close to hating her." So Donna packed her bags and left. "I ain't been back home since. And has it got better? It's gotten better. Okay, a whole lot better. But it didn't get better until I gave my life to Jesus Christ," smiled Donna. "Everything she did to me made me stronger. I'm a survivor."

2

"I REALLY DIDN'T WANT
TO GIVE UP MY KID"

The year was 1978, and she was groggy, stumbling into the women's examination room with the help of a white male doctor and two white female nurses. She had been sedated with local anesthesia, even though she told them emphatically to knock her out cold, which they were unable to do because of the weight she was carrying on her curvy frame.

"Do you want to hear music?" they asked. The room was small and bare and cold. A radio sat atop a desk in the far-left corner, and one of the nurses had clicked on the music. The examination table Donna was lying on was hard, and then she suddenly realized that no, she did not want to go through with the abortion. She wanted what would be her second child and only son, but she couldn't speak. Every time she opened her mouth to say "nooooo, stooooop," nothing but gibberish came out. Then they turned on the machine, which made the loud sucking noise of a vacuum cleaner, and Donna became desperate. "Noooooo, stoooooop," she mouthed again, as the nurses and doctor continued. Cold air blew underneath her back and into her bones as Donna began to shiver. She was terrified, confused. She never did feel the machine go inside of her, but she did hear the sucking noise grow louder and suddenly stop, as if something had been removed. Donna cried.

The recovery room was much larger than the examination room. There were three beds, all filled with women of color. To Donna's left lay a middle-aged Black woman conversing casually. And to that woman's left, a young Latina girl talked excitedly about a big party she planned to attend later that day. Donna stared across the room in a daze. She was torn apart by guilt. Her Catholic upbringing taught her that what she had done was morally reprehensible and a sin against God. "I really didn't see anyone crying," sobbed Donna. "I just wish I could have said firmly, 'Okay, I'm gonna have this child.' The abortion kept me from sleeping for so many years. Oh God, I was so hurt. I really didn't want to give up my kid."

Donna's eyes began to well up with tears as we discussed what it was like to be a Black teenage mother in the city of Boston.

Her voice became higher than usual, and she began to rock her body back and forth as if attempting to soothe an invisible wound in her belly. She believed the child she aborted two years after giving birth to Alexis would have been her only son. "I am ashamed, and I have asked every day for God to forgive me," she sobbed. "This is so painful, Onaje."

Although Donna did not have any sons, her sister Maya had given birth to a beautiful boy earlier, who the family named Timothy. Timmy, as his Aunty Donna referred to him, was active with boundless energy, and Donna wanted to give him the love she wished for her own son. In fact, Timmy spent so much quality time with his aunty that when he became a teenager, he often confided in Donna about the dangers of growing up as a young Black boy in the streets of Boston. There were street gangs on every corner in parts of Dorchester and Roxbury's urban neighborhoods, and as Timmy got older, his mother and aunts began to fear for his safety.

Finally, Maya, who had seen enough violence in the streets, decided it would be better to move her son to Atlanta, where there were more economic opportunities for young people of color. When Timmy found out, he begged his mom to allow him to stay, so he could remain with his childhood friends and family. After some tense family discussions, Maya relented, so long as Timmy promised to live with Donna and visit his mother often in Atlanta.

Secretly, when Donna heard the news, she was overjoyed. "It was like having my own son with me." For a whole year, Donna doted on Timmy, cooking his meals, making his bed, giving him advice about girls and his growing body, and watching him become a young man. At the same time, she did feel guilty, knowing full well Maya was missing her little boy. So one day she finally pulled Timmy aside and said, "Your mother needs you. Your mother's on her own, and she needs you, Timmy."

"Aunty Donna, I don't wanna go back down there," begged Timmy. "But you have a mom, you're not gonna be alone," she assured him, eventually convincing him to move permanently to the ATL.

One morning, a few months after sending Timmy south, Donna couldn't find the strength to get out of bed. "Every time I woke up, I kept falling back to sleep. Then I kept stammering in my sleep, 'God, what's wrong? What's the matter? Why you want me to go to sleep?'" she muttered as she lay in her bed. "I would try to stay awake, but I couldn't. By the time I woke up, it was about seven in the evening, and my phone had been shut off the whole time. I wandered to the corner store for an ice cream and then planted myself on the couch to watch TV. 'Donna! Donna!' I heard my other sister, Stella, screaming outside of my window. 'Hey sis, what's up?' I yelled. 'Did you hear about Timmy?' she asked. 'What about Timmy?' I said. 'I told him yesterday that I was gonna call him today, and I have the phone in my hand. I was about to dial him and talk to him on the phone.'" Donna begins sobbing again as she speaks to me in her living room.

Stella rushed up several flights of stairs to Donna's apartment. "Donna, did you hear what happened with Timmy?"

"No, what happened to Timmy?! I've had the phone in my hand," Donna panicked.

"He got shot," Stella screamed.

"What? What do you mean he got shot? What are you talking about?" Donna demanded, as the pain of the news became unbearable. "What are you talking about?" Donna asked again. "In my mind, I'm saying, 'No, not my Timmy, not my Timmy!'"

"Donna, yes he got shot," insisted Stella. "He was shot in the head." At the sound of those words, Donna screamed and collapsed at the entrance to her apartment door. And as Donna and I spoke about this incident, while sitting at her kitchen table, she began to cry as if she was back in that entrance, just learning her Timmy had been murdered. "Why did you do that to my nephew?" she bawled. "He shot my nephew in the head. He was only fourteen years old. He was only fourteen. He wanted to be a brain surgeon. Oh my God." Unable to console Donna, her sister called an ambulance to the apartment, which took Donna to the hospital and had her sedated.

"Why did this boy kill my nephew? Why did he take my nephew? When he shot my nephew, he took my hopes and dreams. I was watching Timmy live his life when I didn't have my son. I was living through him, and this kid just took my Timmy."

Several days after Timmy's murder, his mother, Maya, flew him back to Boston in a casket for burial. At the funeral home, Donna took a few moments to peer at his lifeless body, noticing his forehead, where the undertaker had pieced back parts of his shattered skull. Once the funeral ended, Donna stepped outside for some fresh air and noticed her other nephew, an eight year old boy named Brandon, escorting a little girl through the funeral home parking lot.

"Why won't Timmy wake up?" the young girl asked Brandon.

"Because he's in heaven with God," sighed Brandon. "He isn't here with us anymore."

Donna thought it was a sweet gesture for little Brandon to console his friend. What she couldn't have known at the time was that a year later, in Boston, Brandon would be murdered, on Halloween, his ninth birthday.

Donna's second nephew Brandon was murdered in the Academy Homes Projects, a government housing community and territory belonging to one of Boston's most violent gangs. When Donna first mentioned Academy Homes to me, the words stopped me cold. As a young man growing up in Roxbury, I knew Academy Homes as a ruthless gang territory entered by very few young people who didn't live there or have a close connection to the gang members repping that block. Academy Homes was located directly across the street from the Heath Street Projects, where my friend, Smiley, whom I mentioned earlier, had been a gang member. Every so often members from one of the two gangs would cross the street and spray bullets indiscriminately into their rival's turf, the hot steel whizzing by the apartment buildings, children's playgrounds, and basketball courts, indifferent to the innocent lives destroyed along the way.

Even though I never dared to walk through Academy Homes, I did know one of the gang's leaders. I came to know Spain on the METCO bus, just as I had become fond of Smiley. Our young, black and brown faces made the journey together each morning to Newton South High School. Spain was a bright and handsome boy with smooth chocolate skin, an infectious smile, and thick braids falling down the side of his head that seemed appropriate for a person with such a strong, but humble leadership presence. I could also tell that Spain was brilliant, especially by the way he answered questions in English class, always thinking outside the box, never caught off guard by our white teachers who cared about Spain but understood him little.

I watched Spain wield that same quick-witted intelligence in the streets, where at a young age he became one of Academy Homes's gang leaders. I'll never forget the day I walked by a house party on Walnut Avenue in Roxbury, almost directly across the street from Malcolm X's half-sister's home, and saw a group of at least thirty young men trooping down the avenue, rocking their shoulders from side-to-side in unison, mouths silent, heads held high, sauntering with the swagger of alleyway cats. I stood mesmerized as my eyes scanned the back of the mass of young boys and men until I reached the front, where, to my surprise, I saw Spain leading the entire group, positioned at the tip of the massive spear of the gang's power. Our eyes met briefly, but I'm not quite sure if Spain ever noticed me or would acknowledge me if he did, which would have brought me unwanted attention. I remember distinctly, though, the glimmer of confidence in his eyes, the fearless intelligence seeping from his pores, and the smirk on his handsome face as he parted the streets.

Years later, as I was pursuing my graduate studies at Boston University, and before I learned about Smiley's execution on the floor of his apartment, I heard troubling news about Spain, too. He had shot a woman in her ankle, and the Boston Police had a warrant out for his arrest. On the run, he hooked up with Paul, another young man I knew from Roxbury, who had recently shot his girlfriend and killed her two best friends in Atlanta. One afternoon in Boston, the police discovered Paul and Spain sleeping in a gray Honda near the Chestnut Hill shopping mall, hiding in plain sight. Spain stepped on the gas, but two cruisers barricaded the street. Both young men leapt from the vehicle. Paul was shot in the leg and caught by the officers almost immediately, while Spain escaped by carjacking the vehicle of an older woman and then speeding away from the scene. Several months later the police caught up with him, cornering him in an apartment building in Roxbury close to where I was raised. Spain told the officers he wasn't going to jail and then, according to official reports, turned the pistol on himself and pulled the trigger.

Donna's nine year old nephew, Brandon, went innocently trick-or-treating in such an environment. As only a little boy could, he bounced around to different apartments in Academy Homes, searching for the best candy and chocolate bars with a big smile on his face. He had spent the past couple of weeks helping elderly people carry groceries to their cars over by Phil's corner supermarket to save up enough money to buy his scary Jason mask, which he wore proudly as he ran up to each door yelling, "Trick or treat!" Brandon made sure to put some of the candy in his pocket when the sound of gunshots blasted through the apartment complex, startling the throngs of kids and adults out for a night of fun. Some children dropped immediately to the ground. Others ran into apartment buildings to escape the bullets ricocheting off the concrete. Brandon ran into his neighbor's apartment and dove under a table while his brother Javon ran upstairs. The loud crack of the pistols subsided. In a panic, the adults frantically inspected every inch of their children's bodies, turning them from side to side, up and down and over, hoping to find their children unharmed. Then someone saw that Brandon was holding his hands over his stomach—a bullet hole had ripped open his belly. Another person frantically flagged down an ambulance that happened to be cruising down Columbus Avenue near the Academy Homes, so EMTs could rush Brandon out of the apartment and onto a stretcher. Laying there with blood running from his stomach, Brandon turned to the first responder and asked where his candy was.

"Donna, you've gotta go on a bus to Boston Medical Center, your nephew Brandon got shot!" Donna's mother Olivia screamed over the phone, giving Donna the news that her second nephew in a year was on the verge of dying.

"Brandon? No! Ma, you're mistaken! Only nine," Donna sobbed. She looked over at her apartment bathroom, where Brandon's sister was about to take a shower. She hung up the phone and placed her back against the bathroom door, unsure of the proper words to say.

"Sweetie, we've got to leave, we've gotta go to the hospital because your brother just got shot." Brandon's older sister jumped out of the shower, and the two of them ran out into the cold, penniless and unable to pay for a taxi to get to the hospital on time. "Please take me to Boston Medical Center, my nephew just got shot, he's nine years old," Donna begged a taxi driver.

"Ma'am, no problem, just get in the car," he said.

At Boston Medical Center, Brandon's mother, Stella, was hysterical. She begged the doctors to allow Donna to speak to Brandon before they wheeled him into surgery. Stella counted on her sister to comfort him and ease his fear. "My family leans on me in times of tragedy," cried Donna as we spoke.

"Don't let him go without my sister seeing him!" screamed Stella. But Donna could only see the hurried look on the doctors' faces before Brandon was out of reach.

In the waiting room, the entire family huddled together and prayed, kneeling on the floor. Donna looked up and spotted the grief counselor entering the room, a tear rolling down her face. When Stella realized what was happening, she stood up and walked into the hallway. "You need to go in there and tell my sister! You need to go in there and tell my sister and you need to tell her now. Don't give my sister false hope. Go in there and tell her!" Donna screamed at the grief counselor.

The grief counselor approached Stella. "They don't think Brandon is going to make it." At that, Stella turned and bolted out of the hospital doors and down Harrison Avenue, nearly getting hit in the bustling traffic.

"Please, somebody please go get her!" Donna pleaded, as the family fell apart on the hospital floor. An observing stranger sprinted out of the room and down the street, catching Stella and carrying her back to Boston Medical.

"God no, please not again, not another son!" sobbed Donna. The surgeons entered the room, and they too fell to the ground with the family, weeping about how they had struggled to save little Brandon's life.

"Oh, my Lord, I've never seen so much pain," sobbed Donna, echoing the psychologist Esther J. Jenkins's study of Black women's experiences of community violence, trauma, and grief: "The murder of a child is among the most difficult traumas to deal with. It represents 'multiple losses of both a real and symbolic nature.' . . . Some parents will lose another child to death . . . the same environmental factors that contributed to the death of one child have the potential for claiming other offspring."[1]

That same evening, the family was given the opportunity to view Brandon's body at the hospital. "This stuff was in his pockets," whispered the grief counselor to Donna as she pulled her aside and showed her the Mickey and Minnie Mouse rings, three single dollar bills, and the candy Brandon had secured neatly in his jeans. "I think you all would want it."

Donna held Brandon's belongings in her hands and examined the shirt he had been wearing, a gaping hole in the center stained with blood. "How was he supposed to survive with a hole that big in his stomach?" she asked through tears.

Stella couldn't breathe and was quickly given oxygen by the medical staff. "Stella, these were in Brandon's pocket. He would want you to have them," Donna said as she handed some of the items to her sister. She then looked over at her mother, Olivia, who was staring at the ceiling in a daze.

"Where's Brandon? Where's my grandson?" mumbled Olivia.

"Mommy, this was in Brandon's pockets, and I think Brandon would want you to have it," Donna said, trying to comfort her.

"Donna, it really happened?" replied a bewildered Olivia.

"Yes, Mom, Brandon's no longer with us."

Donna's was a family of Black women in the waiting room of Boston Medical Hospital suffering from multiple losses and "continuous traumatic stress."[2]

As Donna and I huddled around her plain wooden table in the middle of her living room, deep lines formed on her forehead as she remembered the deaths of her nephews and unborn son. She squeezed her wet eyes open and shut and rocked back and forth on the creaky wooden chair.

To this day, the scars caused by Brandon's death continue to ache within Donna's family and Roxbury's community as a whole. The EMTs who tried to save Brandon's life felt compelled to honor his memory in some physical way, so they built a makeshift shrine near the location of his murder, posting a large white sign and flowers against a tree next to the sidewalk. Every year on Brandon's favorite day, Halloween, his birthday, the EMTs visit the scene of his murder to honor the nine-year-old boy. The shrine reads: "We Do Not Forget. To the Memory of Brandon and so many ~ that we wish we had never known ~ The EMTs and Medics of Boston EMS."

As I sat there in Donna's living room, I couldn't find the words to express the pain I felt for her and her sisters, whose bodies and children had been under assault in America for most of their lives. I remained silent, humbled by Donna's vulnerability. She shared her life with me as if I were her own child.

"You won't believe me, but I was your mother in a previous life," I remembered her saying on the first day we met. "I wasn't the way I was supposed to be, and I steered you away from your true purpose the last time. But now I am the way God wants me to be, and we are meeting now so I can steer you in the right direction this time."

Donna had lost her son in 1978, two years before I was born in Boston, and according to her, we were from the same African lineage. Like Toni Morrison's Sethe, did Donna believe that I had returned to her home with the soul of her beloved boy?[3] All I knew for sure was that Donna saw our interviews as a second chance to mother a son that been taken.

As a result, I began to see our ethnographic collaboration through a new lens. In the world we were creating together, Donna was not an object of scientific investigation for me to reveal through analysis, nor did she see me as an outside observer determined to strip her of agency. Rather, we had formed an "intermediate realm . . . at once both subjective and objective without being exclusively either."[4] This intersubjective place between us, which allowed for an alternative experience of temporality, the presence of ancestors and other unseen spirits, including the life force of her aborted son flowing through my veins, became the site where we were configuring academic knowledge about Donna's lived religion.[5]

In this sense, Donna and I were producing a living "archive of conjure."

> [These] archives are particularly thorny sites littered with bits of bones of unfinished narratives that may or may not reveal points of encounter between layered pasts and spiritual protagonists. They echo with the voices of partially accessible and imperfect ancestors. Archives of conjure produce these ancestors through a scholarly practice that engages in a kind of spirit mediumship that moves the production of knowledge to a collaborative plane much like the spiritist séance. Polyvocality, temporal overlapping, and the nagging yet necessary voice of the skeptic are conjoined.[6]

After I became aware of the spectral presence of Donna's aborted son in our interviews, I contacted a knowledgeable expert in the Yoruba Òrìsà traditions of the African Diaspora to better understand at least one African religious tradition's conception of reincarnation. "There is some speculation by our African elders," the informant explained, "that when a child is aborted, it breaks the contract between that soul and the immediate family within which he or she had agreed to be born. After the abortion, the child may choose a different branch within the larger spiritual family [tree]."[7]

Might I possess the soul of her son who had chosen another family in Roxbury with similar Afro-Jamaican roots two years after Donna's abortion? I decided to raise this possibility with Donna. "Yes," she said. "I'm glad you came back to me, my son."

3

"AM I EVER GOING TO
BE NORMAL?"

I n a situation of poverty and racial exclusion, the impact of teenage pregnancy, sexual abuse, and depression can be compounded by the presence of failing schools, which further create a sense of foreshortened future for girls such as Donna. The intersection of racism, sexism, and poverty uniquely position Black girls to be overlooked, underprotected, and pushed out of the U.S. educational system in rates disproportionate to those for other students.[1] For Donna, these factors were compounded by the presence of a learning disability, which, because it went undetected, amplified her feelings of invisibility. Although she didn't know it at the time, Donna experienced lead poisoning as a child, probably from eating crusty blue paint chips crumbling off of her mother's apartment walls and from inhaling the dust that gathered in filthy stairwells. However, rather than receiving the proper attention and testing as she struggled in school, Donna was simply characterized as "slow" by her mother and her teachers, an attribute she ultimately accepted.

"My mom could tell that I was a little slow, and I always felt like I had to catch up in school. It was always extra hard for me, I mean so hard, and I never made it to a B or an A. I always had a C or a C+. I can't even believe that I graduated out of the eighth grade. I never copied people's work, and I had no one ever to help me, and when I asked my mom to help me, she was like, 'Sit down and do it!' But unbeknownst to me, my mother didn't complete her education either," sighed Donna.

For the first three years of her elementary education, none of Donna's teachers found the time to offer her extra support. Instead, like Ralph Ellison's *Invisible Man*, they simply chose not to see her, passing her from one grade to the next, though she had failed her subjects the previous year.[2] It wasn't until Donna reached the fifth grade that she was fortunate enough to enter the classroom of Mrs. Murphy, the first teacher in her life who seemed to recognize her unique challenges.

Unlike Donna's previous teachers, Mrs. Murphy was a cool white woman married to a Black man and seemed to have a genuine connection to the community she taught. It was the 1960s, and Mrs. Murphy wore a hippie bead necklace, parted her long red hair in the middle, and drove a Volkswagen beetle from her white Irish neighborhood to teach in Boston's Black inner-city schools.

"She was the first teacher that didn't make me feel stupid in her class. She accepted me," remembered an emotional Donna. And when Mrs. Murphy noticed that Donna was learning at a

slower pace than other students, she had the gumption to follow
Donna to her Housing Projects to meet with her mother, Olivia,
in person.

"Ms. Haskins, do you mind if I take your Donna home
with me after school some days to give her extra support?"
Mrs. Murphy asked Olivia.

"Sure, baby. That's nice of you. Just make sure you have her
home at a decent time," Olivia responded gratefully.

The first day Mrs. Murphy took Donna to her nice suburban
home, the two immediately sat down at her kitchen table, directly
across from the living room. Mrs. Murphy then placed a series
of reading tests in front of Donna to identify whether she could
read basic words for a fifth grader. When Donna couldn't read
or spell all the words on the page, she looked up into Mrs. Murphy's eyes and broke down, sobbing over her kitchen table. "She
knew off the bat that I didn't know how to spell. And I sat there,
and I just broke down and cried, and she said, 'Donna, I'm going
to help you.'"

So for the next several months, almost every day after school,
Mrs. Murphy brought Donna to her home to study, even
sometimes driving to the Projects to pick her up on the week-
ends. And for a while Donna felt like she was part of the
Murphy family, babysitting Mrs. Murphy's youngest daughter
and becoming quite fond of Mr. Murphy. "I learned a lot from
Mrs. Murphy," Donna recalled. "You know what she told me
one time, Onaje? She sat me down and said, 'Donna, you can do
it. Don't be afraid to learn. You can do it.' She was the best
teacher I ever had," beamed Donna. "But then, she was a fifth-
grade teacher. I had to go to the sixth grade."

Unfortunately, in the sixth grade, Donna sunk back into invisibility. In fact, she felt so unsafe and overlooked in her new
classroom that she sometimes waited patiently in the school

hallways for a chance to see Mrs. Murphy again. As soon as Donna spotted her long red hair flowing down the corridor, she'd run up to Mrs. Murphy excitedly and fall into her arms. And when Donna occasionally found the courage to ask Mrs. Murphy for help with her schoolwork, Mrs. Murphy would quickly usher the two of them into a school supply closet where they could work privately without Donna feeling embarrassed by the peering eyes of her classmates. Working with Donna in the closet also protected Mrs. Murphy from disciplinary action by the school administrators for offering extra help to a sixth-grade student. Nevertheless, as the school year progressed, she ran into Mrs. Murphy less and less, until eventually she stopped seeing her at school altogether. Donna told herself that Mrs. Murphy probably quit the school or maybe her beloved teacher just didn't have the resources and time to help her anymore. Regardless of the reason, Donna believed she was alone, with no choice but to return to pretending to learn in her sixth-grade class.

Donna fell through the cracks over the next several years. She would simply sit in her classrooms pretending to learn, and her teachers would play along, graduating her to the next grade. And on the rare occasion that her teacher would hold her back a year, she would repeat the process, only to move up a grade the following year without any measurable improvement. "I would have to sit in the class and pretend that I knew the work, and I didn't know the work, so I faked my way. I did what I knew, and what I didn't know, I didn't. Sixth grade, seventh grade, same way."

The sixth grade was especially difficult for Donna. Ms. Foster was Donna's teacher in the sixth grade, and the students in her class were some of the brightest in the entire school. One day Ms. Foster called on Donna to solve a multiplication problem on the board in front of the class. As soon as Donna pushed back her chair to stand up, the entire class erupted in hands-over-mouth, slap-knee laughter. Donna slowly inched her way to the front, head down, staring at the language of numbers on the chalkboard for a while, before she began to scratch the green surface with the smooth chalk. When Donna finally took her hands away from the board, the class was shocked. She had gotten the answer correct!

"I worked harder than anyone in that classroom because I had to work twice as hard," Donna shook her head in frustration. It was one of the few bright moments—if you can call being mocked a good moment—that she remembered as a student. And sure enough, at the end of the year, Ms. Foster graduated Donna to the seventh grade, even though she remained unable to read and write beyond the level of a fifth grader. Donna's seventh- and eighth-grade teachers also passed her even though she was unable to read, so that when she walked across the stage and received her middle school diploma, she didn't feel a sense of accomplishment or joy. Her graduation was confirmation that no one cared.

"When I graduated and got an eighth-grade diploma, I was literally shocked. And I figured that they just graduated me just to get me out of there, knowing I didn't know how to do the work."

When Donna matriculated to the ninth grade, she couldn't fake her way through school anymore. The level of difficulty of high school work was too much, and she didn't want to be a victim of Boston's deeply segregated school system's culture of passing any longer.[3] She was already an eighteen-year-old ninth grader. So Olivia decided to send Donna to a unique school in Brookline, Massachusetts, called New Perspective, which at the time was designed to address the unique needs of formerly underserved students in the Boston public school system. In the beginning, New Perspective did meet Donna's special needs. She was fortunate enough to meet another wonderful teacher with a

big heart like Mrs. Murphy, and this time, her teacher sus-
pected Donna had a diagnosable learning disability—although
strangely, she never had Donna formally tested. Instead, Donna's new teacher offered her help after school and demonstrated
a few reading techniques to help her comprehend words better
on the page. But given that the school had no formal special education classes, Donna only slightly improved. By the end of the
school year, when she took her reading exam, she still read at
the level of a fifth grader, right where Mrs. Murphy had left off.
When Donna found out her score, the sense of shame devas-
tated her.

"I can't do it anymore," she said to herself, deciding to drop
out of school altogether, around the same time that she had
become pregnant with Alexis, her first child.

As a teenager preparing to have a daughter of her own, Donna
felt her self-esteem crushed by the sting of not knowing how to
read, of being unable to decipher the markings on a page in a
way that gave meaning to the world around her. And yet, in subsequent years, even after surviving her attempted suicide, har-
boring guilt over her abortion, and losing her two nephews to
murder, Donna still found the courage to get tested to measure
her reading level and to enroll in one of Boston's free adult literacy programs in the hopes of creating a better life for her family. The initial tests came back as she predicted—she was still
reading at the level of a fifth grader. But this time, as an adult,
Donna felt that if she threw herself into her classes, reviewing
vocabulary words each evening and arriving to class on time, she
could finally succeed. And most important, she started to believe
in her intellectual abilities for the first time.

"I didn't say to myself, 'No, I can't do this,' which is what I
often told myself as a child." Instead, Donna seemed to be

internalizing the advice Mrs. Murphy had given her in the fifth grade.

"You can do it Donna. Don't be afraid to learn." And for a while it worked. Donna made it successfully to the end of the class, where she was required to take the final writing exam that would indicate whether she was ready to earn her general equivalency diploma (GED).

On the day of the exam, Donna sat anxiously at her desk, staring at the teacher as she handed out to students a single sheet of white paper on which Donna was to write a story of her choosing. As the crisp sheet landed on her desk, Donna picked up her pencil and began to write. She finished her first sentence with a triumphant period and smiled, but then, as she began to write the second sentence, she realized something. She had completely forgotten what she had written before. How could she write a second sentence if it had no relation to the previous one? So she reread her first sentence a few times, hoping the repetition would imprint the thoughts. But by the time she placed her pencil on the page, she had forgotten the first sentence all over again. Donna sighed and started writing again anyway, each time starting a new sentence by forgetting the old one, so that when she had enough sentences to form a paragraph, it read as a disjointed, chaotic mishmash of words on the page. When the exam was over, Donna stood up quickly, handed her white sheet of paper to the teacher, and walked out of the classroom.

Donna dreaded the afternoon she was required to return to class to pick up her results, but instead of giving her a grade, her teacher pulled her aside to talk privately. "Donna, there's this place over near Charles River Park. You should get yourself tested for a disability." Donna's self-esteem was crushed all over again. But in desperation to figure out why she was unable to read and write like everyone else, she followed her instructor's advice and immediately walked over to Charles River Park to get tested.

"I go to the Charles River Park, and after the test is all over, he tells me that I'm dyslexic. He said, 'You have the disability that Bill Cosby's son had, the one that died, that whatever I see in my head won't come out on paper, that I will have to recheck it, reverse it, and recheck it."

The news of her learning disability left Donna feeling hopeless. For the second time in her life, she was prepared to commit suicide. "I got really down that day. I got so down that day. I stood on the bridge where the walkway crosses the highway, and I just stood there gazing down at the road. I just wanted to jump. I wanted to just end it all right there. What stopped me is I had to go to the courthouse that day, to watch the trial of Brandon's murderer. In my mind, I was saying, 'Am I ever going to be normal? Why do I have to have this? Why can't I be like everyone else? Why does it have to be so hard for me?' And I kept pursuing and pursuing my education, kept trying to get that diploma."

Even in her early forties, Donna forced herself to take another literacy class, this time in the Mission Hill area of Roxbury, though she already knew she couldn't pass. As she moped hopelessly toward the learning center, Donna suddenly heard a mysterious voice out of nowhere.

"Accept who you are, and I will," advised an unseen presence. Donna turned around but didn't see anyone. "Accept who you are, and I will," the apparition urged again. However, rather than panicking, Donna felt a strange calmness come over her, which she would later attribute to the Holy Spirit. Donna turned away from the learning center and went home instead. Once in her apartment, she opened the door and sat down in her silent living room—and heard the voice a third time.

"Haven't I brought you all the way here? Haven't I brought you? Haven't I brought you here? Trust me. Trust me, and I will take you the rest of the way."

From that moment onward, Donna decided let go of her dream to be literate, and to their pleasant surprise, her children noticed a growing sense of ease in her. "They were like, 'Ma, you're not going,' and I told them like it was. I still stand by what I heard from the Holy Spirit. Some people might not understand it, but I stand by His word. He said, 'Trust me,' and I trust him. Do I still have trouble spelling? Yes, but it's not a handicap for me because I know what I can do to remember words. And I prayed, I said, 'Father, you don't want me to go to school, then you've got to create me a new mind. Give me a new mind. Give me new wisdom. And people keep asking me, 'Don't you want the diploma?' But see, God wanted me to get a diploma from the kingdom of Heaven. That's where He wanted me to get my degree."

Through her struggle to become literate within the racially segregated labyrinth of the Boston public school system, Donna stumbled on a powerful epistemological insight. Consciousness of "the things behind the things"—otherworldly voices and unearthly ghosts—rests beyond the myopic constructions of written language. "In the culture of my people," Malidoma Patrice Some, Dagara shaman and scholar of African religions, writes, "we have no word for the supernatural. The closest we come to this concept is *Yielbongura*, 'The thing that knowledge cannot eat.' This word suggests that the life and power of certain [fantastic] things depend upon their resistance to the kind of categorizing knowledge that human beings apply to everything."[4]

Might Donna's inability to reduce life to the arbitrary restraints of the written word have been the result of her openness to the supernatural? I wondered. After all, hadn't other prophets been illiterate too?[5]

"And I would not tell anybody to drop out of school," cautioned Donna. "No. All our journeys are different. But I'm saying that's how it is for me. Eventually the Holy Spirit would grant Donna a diploma from heaven, giving her a new mind aware of "things that knowledge cannot eat"—but first the continuous onslaught of gender-based violence in Boston's neigborhoods stood in her way.[6]

4

"EVERY TIME YOU LEAVE, YOU TAKE A PIECE OF ME WITH YOU"

Donna didn't love the father of her first child. She chose to sleep with Cornell because she wanted their baby to give her the love she wasn't receiving at home. "It was like me trying to reincarnate myself," she explained. "I could take care of that child how I wanted to be raised. I was going to show my mother how a child should be raised."

Donna met Cornell during her first and only year at New Perspective School in Brookline. Her ninth-grade classes were in the evenings, so around nine o'clock, she would board the number sixty-six MBTA bus from Brookline to Dudley Station in Roxbury and then take the number eight bus from Dudley to the Point in Dorchester. Then she'd walk up three flights of stairs to her mother's apartment, usually in a dejected mood.

That's when Cornell entered the frame. He was dark, muscular, and tall, and he gave Donna the attention she craved. He lived with his sister across the hallway from Donna's mother's apartment, and one evening, he happened to open his door just as Donna was making her way home from school. After that, Cornell took every opportunity to flirt with her. "Why you always spending time with Puerto Rican boys?" he'd ask her when he saw her coming home from school. "Don't you like Black boys like me? You look so pretty today, girl."

Donna knew that Cornell already had a girlfriend, but she also loved the attention. And she was pleasantly surprised one evening when she entered her mother's apartment and found Cornell at the kitchen table playing a card game of spades with Olivia and her sisters. Olivia loved to play spades in the evenings, and she didn't just let anyone sit at her kitchen table, especially a young potential suiter to one of her girls. Donna was impressed. If Cornell was smooth enough to curry favor with Olivia, he must be exceptionally gallant, she thought.

Donna and Cornell courted each other in this roundabout way for several months, until one evening, after a game of spades, Cornell invited Donna over to his apartment under the pretense of watching a Major League Baseball game featuring the Boston Red Sox. Once the two friends entered Cornell's apartment, they sat on the living room couch for a few minutes in front of the television before they made their way to Cornell's bedroom. Cornell closed the door behind them and sat on the bed while Donna remained standing. She was flooded with emotions. Attracted? Yes. Wanting a baby? Yes. Guilty that he had a girlfriend? Yes. Donna turned around and put her hand on the doorknob to leave, but it was locked from the inside. She turned toward Cornell, who was laying on the bed, dangling the key to the door in front of his face as if to say, "you 'ain't going nowhere." She gave in. It was the first of three, almost consecutive evenings they had sex together in Cornell's sister's apartment. It was everything Donna craved.

However, the day after their last encounter, Donna spotted Cornell holding hands with his girlfriend as they kissed and walked down the street in the Point. "They were hugged up," Donna recalls, and it broke her heart, even enraged her. She was so angry, in fact, she went looking around the projects for her Puerto Rican boyfriend, Pablo, and had unprotected revenge sex with him that evening, deciding she was done with spending time with Cornell for good.

However, several days later, Donna wasn't feeling so good down around her private parts and confided to a close friend about experiencing a strange discharge and painful urination. Her friend advised her to visit Boston City Hospital immediately. So the next day she snuck her mother's Medicaid card from her purse and took the bus to get tested for gonorrhea. At the hospital, the nurse confirmed what Donna already knew. She was positive for gonorrhea and needed a shot to prevent the illness from progressing.

"Donna, this shot should take care of the gonorrhea," the nurse advised. "We will administer it today, just as long as you are not pregnant. There is a chance of blindness to an unborn child if a pregnant mother is given this treatment. Are you pregnant?"

"No," Donna answered. "I'm not pregnant." Even though it was possible she had conceived with Cornell or Pablo, Donna told herself there was no way she could actually be having a baby.

However, Donna panicked a month later when she didn't see her period. She felt nauseous and couldn't get out of bed in time for school at New Perspective. She confided in her friend again, who offered similar advice: "Go to the hospital and get tested." It was October 1975, and the first early home pregnancy tests wouldn't be approved by the FDA until 1977, so Donna again made her way to Boston City Hospital and then waited at home with her girlfriend until the afternoon to call for results.

"I'm calling for a pregnancy test for Donna Haskins," she said on the phone to the hospital.

"Do you want the good news or bad news?" the nurse asked.

"The good news," Donna replied.

"The good news is you won't see your period for another nine months. The bad news is, you're pregnant," the nurse said wryly. Donna hung up the phone.

"I can't be. I can't be," Donna repeated as she pictured her mother's face.

"Your mother's going to kill you," her girlfriend blurted out, as if reading Donna's mind.

Donna spent the next several days wishing away her pregnancy, as if not talking about her unborn child would make it disappear. Then one morning her sister Stella caught Donna vomiting in the bathroom. "You better not be pregnant. Mom is going to kill you! Yo gotta tell Mommy!" said Stella.

A few days later Donna came home from school and plopped down at the kitchen table next to her mother, who was playing spades with two of her sisters and some family friends. Someone dealt Donna into the game, and she immediately smiled at the hand she had been given, knowing if she played her cards right, she'd probably score the highest number of books that round. Just as Donna got good and comfortable, Stella walked in.

"Mom, I just want you to know, somebody at the kitchen table is pregnaaaaaant!" Stella teased. Donna's face sunk behind her hand full of aces. Olivia looked up from her own cards in disbelief.

"Stella, you better stop playing!" she said.

"Mom, I'm serious, somebody here is pregnaaaaaant!" Stella repeated.

"Who?!" Dorothy asked as she looked around the table at each of her girls and a teenage neighbor. "Maya, is it you?!"

"No Ma, I ain't pregnant!" Maya pleaded her innocence.

"Dora, is it you!?" Olivia asked her other daughter.

"No Ma, it ain't me!" assured Dora.

Then Olivia turned to the young girl who was visiting. "You, Ashley?!"

"No, I definitely ain't pregnant, uh!"

"Stella?! You?!" Olivia's piercing eyes landed on Stella.

"Ma, if I was pregnant, would I have just told you?"

Donna held onto her cards for dear life as everybody in the room slowly turned to look at her, including Olivia, who had been sitting right next to her the whole time. "Donna, no, not my Donna!" Olivia started crying once the look of guilt washed across Donna's face. Her stepfather Noah, who had been sitting at the table the whole time, quickly ushered all the girls and guests out of the apartment, except Donna.

"Your mother and I have to have a conversation with Donna. Please leave."

Donna stood up and ran into her mother's bedroom, with Olivia chasing close behind, screaming and crying. "You better not hit her, Olivia," Noah yelled down the corridor. "Your mother kicked you out when you had Stella at eighteen years old. You going to do that to Donna now?"

Those words stopped Olivia in her tracks once she reached the bedroom. Her daughter was repeating the mistakes she had made as a teenager. "No, I'm not going to kick you out of my house, Donna, but you are going to have this child," exclaimed Olivia, whose Catholic beliefs prohibited abortion. Olivia then turned away from Donna with a look of disgust and walked out of her bedroom. Only Donna's stepfather remained to console her as she wept on the bed.

Noah was the only person in Donna's life over the next few months to show her compassion. When her stomach began to grow, he took her to Zayre to buy her first maternity clothes: two pairs of pants, two tops, and several beautiful dresses. Olivia, on the other hand, couldn't set aside her anger and embarrassment to be there for her daughter. Seeing Donna pregnant at eighteen probably reminded Olivia too much of her own shortcomings. And so she fed Donna good food for the baby but kept her love locked away somewhere deep inside. In fact, the only time Donna ever felt her mother's love was the evening Donna returned to the apartment from the rain after almost having jumped into Dorchester bay to kill herself and her unborn child a few months later. The way Olivia wiped away Donna's tears and stroked her hair and said, "Donna, everything's going to be okay," meant the world to her. That was all Donna ever wanted from her mother, to be loved. To be understood.

Donna was terrified that Cornell might not be the father of her child. She initially told her mother and anyone else who would listen that he was, because she wanted him to be, plus they had sex three times in a week, whereas she only had sex with Pablo once in the same time period, she reasoned. But she knew deep down the baby in her stomach could be Pablo's just the same, and the thought scared her. What if her baby looked like Pablo with curly hair? she thought. Everyone in the neighborhood would know it wasn't Cornell's and call her a ho and a slut and say that she couldn't even name the father of her own baby. And on the other hand, Cornell and Pablo would be hailed as the epitome of masculine virility.

It made the situation even worse that Cornell put the word out in the Point that he wasn't the father of Donna's unborn child. She must have gotten pregnant from some other man, he told his friends and his girlfriend, whom he wanted to make believe that he had never had sex with Donna. When Olivia heard that Cornell was denying Donna's baby, she was beside herself.

"You trying to say my daughter's a liar. You trying to say she's a ho?" Olivia yelled at Cornell one day as she pinned his neck against the door with her bare hands. "You saying she's a ho?" she asked. Donna watched in terrible delight as her mother grasped her baby-father's jugular as someone started banging on the front door. Donna marched over and opened it. The woman on the other side was Cornell's girlfriend. Donna took one look at her and, without saying a word, slammed the door right in her face.

Cornell continued to deny Donna's unborn child, despite Olivia's venom, up until the day she was born. And Donna remained as confused and scared as ever. Not only was she worried that her child might expose her sexual life by coming into the world with Pablo's curly hair, she was also nervous that her baby might be blind from the gonorrhea shot. All these fears flooded Donna's mind as her mucus plug broke and she dashed out of her apartment building to get to the hospital in time to give birth, with Olivia following right behind her. Unfortunately, as Donna hobbled down the stairs, she spotted Cornell and his girlfriend coming up in the opposite direction. The four combatants stared at each other in silence as they passed each other, but then, as Donna and Cornell turned a corner, Olivia reached upward and snatched Cornell's ankle on the staircase above.

"You bastard! You dirty bastard!" she yelled at him, as she tried to yank his ankle clean through the metal bars.

"Come on, Mom!" Donna yelled at her mother, as she struggled to continue down the steps.

"You dirty bastard. You should be going with her!" Olivia screamed at Cornell before finally letting go and following her daughter to the street outside.

Once Donna reached the hospital, she immediately went into labor. After thirteen intense hours, she gave birth to a beautiful baby girl with reddish skin and coal-black hair, whom she named Alexis.

"How's her eyesight?" Donna asked her doctor.

"Her eyes look just fine," the doctor assured Donna to her relief. With Alexis's reddish skin, Donna couldn't be sure if the baby was Cornell's, but at least her hair wasn't curly, and she wasn't blind. Holding Alexis in her arms for the first time washed away all her fears for the moment.

A few days later, when Donna was allowed to take Alexis home, she entered her mother's apartment to find the floors waxed and spotless, the apartment decorated, and the cabinets full of formula and diapers, courtesy of her mother. Noah even bought Donna a beautiful purple crib. And when Donna saw Olivia hold Alexis in her arms for the first time, she thought, "You're going to give this baby the love I never had."

Cornell, however, was a different story. He continued to deny Alexis and after three months still had not stopped by to see her. Donna didn't much care, because it was her plan all along to raise Alexis by herself, but Olivia and Noah were livid.

"Look at your daughter!" Noah commanded on the day he brought Cornell into the apartment to see Alexis. When Cornell wouldn't look, Donna's stepfather took his massive hands and turned Cornell's resisting body toward the crib. "Look!"

Cornell finally looked but continued to deny Alexis once he left the apartment, even though, after four months, the baby's skin had darkened and an older neighbor on the first floor kept saying she looked just like Cornell. "Stop lying on Donna," the woman told Cornell each time he passed by. Donna was relieved. Her daughter had perfect eyesight, and now, after four months, she was sure that Alexis wasn't Pablo's.

Olivia was still angry, though, and wouldn't let Cornell rest until he publicly declared himself the father of Donna's baby. "You're taking him to court, Donna," demanded Olivia. "He's going to help you raise this child."

So when Alexis was a year old, Donna took Cornell to Dorchester district court to sue for child support. Cornell's lawyer asked to delay the trial until a blood test was administered to confirm paternity. The judge obliged and gave Cornell a reasonable period to pay for the test. However, when Cornell was unable to produce the paternity test after several months, the judge lost his patience and called both parties to court.

Donna stood next to Cornell, the baby in her arms, and together they faced the judge, but when Alexis went to touch his arm, Cornell jerked it away. The judge exploded. "That is a baby! She didn't do anything to you to deserve this! You're going to pull back from a baby! We are going to trial today!" he screamed.

During the trial, Donna was called to the witness stand by Cornell's attorney, who forced her to repeat the details of her sexual encounters with Cornell. "Yes, we had sex in his sister's house, on his bed, on the nights of September 23rd, 24th, we skipped September 25th, which was my birthday, and we had sex again on September 26th," Donna testified, pulling out a calendar with the words "sex with Cornell" written on each date. Her mother had taught her to keep a calendar of the days she had intercourse and to mark down her period. She submitted the journal as evidence to the court.

"Oh no," the judge intoned. "She's got this thing down pat. She has her dates right. After deliberation, I declare you, Cornell, the father of this child, and you are hereby ordered to pay seventy-five dollars a week to Ms. Donna Haskins in child support."

Donna was vindicated. She had stood up for herself and proven that she wasn't a liar or a slut. As Donna walked out of the courtroom with her mother and stepfather, Olivia turned to Cornell and said: "You going to have your head hanging between your balls. You ain't going to call my daughter a ho."

Donna felt vindicated. "Mommy and Daddy, do you mind if I walk home with Alexis?" she asked, wanting to take in everything that happened to her in the first nineteen years of her life.

"Yes, no problem, Donna. You okay?" her mother asked.

"Yes, Mom, I'm okay," Donna sighed. Donna walked out of the courthouse, the sun shining on her caramel face, and whispered to Alexis: "He may not want to be your Daddy, but I'm going to be your Daddy." Then, in her heart, she thanked her mother, Olivia.

"It's like something changed in my Mom when I had Alexis," she remembered fondly. "I walked all the way from Dorchester courthouse to Dudley Station. And from that moment on, it was just me and my oldest daughter, my pride and joy, and my heart and soul."

SCOOTER

The following year, Donna met Scooter at the annual West Indian festival at Franklin Park, near Blue Hill Avenue, in Roxbury. A neighbor agreed to purchase a bus pass for Donna and her one-year-old daughter, Alexis, so they could attend, since Donna couldn't afford to get there on her own. Once she arrived, Donna was enthralled by the catchy sounds and heavy rhythms of Calypso and Suka and entranced by the spiraling waists, jumping feet, and flowing hands of the Afro-Caribbean dancers who crowned the massive colorful floats moving slowly down the avenue. Donna got herself some savory Jamaican food full of curry and jerk and gave her daughter a little taste, too, as she danced among the crowd of black and brown bodies bustling down Blue Hill Avenue. Toward the end of the day, the carnival floats came to a stop, gathering in one last spot for a symphony of Afro-Caribbean rhythms and dancing, electrifying the crowd of onlookers who had gathered to take all that beauty in. After a while the night energy became too intense for a one-year-old, so Donna decided to make her way out of the crowd and toward the bus stop on Blue Hill Avenue.

That's when Scooter approached Donna, slowly and gracefully dancing over to one of her friends, his sly hips winding back and forth, second in power only to his striking smile. Donna tried to pay him no mind, partly because she had Alexis with her.

"I would like to talk to her," Scooter pointed at Donna confidently as he spoke to her friend. As he approached her, Scooter kept dancing and smiling, and it made Donna laugh. "My name is Scooter," he said holding out his hand like a perfect gentleman. "Can I call you sometime?" he smiled.

Scooter called Donna a few days later, and they spoke on the phone every day after that for two weeks straight. She loved the sound of his voice. "I live with my mother," Donna kept remind-ing Scooter each time he asked to visit her apartment. "If you stop by, you have to respect my mother's house," Donna warned. What she really meant was that the two could not have sex, which was the last thing Donna wanted, given the ordeal she had just been through with Alexis's father. So when Scooter agreed to be a perfect gentleman if Donna allowed him to come over, she relented and gave him her address.

It was raining hard the day Scooter knocked on Donna's door and entered her apartment, wearing that same beautiful smile. Olivia wasn't home, and the two sat on the living room couch and began to talk.

"You are so beautiful," he complimented Donna's blushing face while staring into her eyes.

"Thank you," she responded.

Scooter inched closer. "So beautiful, girl."

At that moment, Donna realized why Scooter had wanted so badly to come over. He didn't just want to talk. "Thank you," she said again. "But listen, let's just talk. I'm not protected. I am not taking birth control pills and don't want to have sex."

"Don't worry, baby, I'll pull out of you. I won't come in you," Scooter promised, as he leaned over Donna's body hard and began to pull down her pants.

"You dirty bastard," Donna shouted, as Scooter entered her without her permission or protection. When Scooter finally got off her, she was angry, scared, and hurt. "I'm pregnant now. I know it. Why did you do that? I didn't want to have sex."

"I'm sorry," begged Scooter. "I didn't mean to. If you do get pregnant, I'll be there for you," he promised.

A month after being raped by him, Donna was pregnant with Scooter's child. "Scooter," Donna said over the phone one evening, "I'm pregnant, and it has to be yours."

"It's not mine, can't be mine," countered Scooter, before hanging up on her. Donna felt ashamed. She was pregnant by another man who denied being the father. She knew everyone in the neighborhood would laugh at her and whisper to each other that she couldn't keep her legs shut. And her mother. The look of disappointment in Olivia's eyes would be enough to kill her, let alone her heavy hands.

"I can't handle this," Donna cried. "I can't have this child. But I'm Catholic."

Several days after finding out she was pregnant, Donna called Karen, her former teacher at New Perspective School in Brookline, the one she had dropped out of a year earlier. "I'm sorry Ms. Karen, but I can't have this baby. Can you take me to the hospital?" she asked.

The following day Ms. Karen picked Donna up at her mother's apartment and brought her to the hospital for an abortion. "I aborted what would have been my only son," Donna cried as she told me this story, reminding me of the child with whom she believed I shared a special bond. "Even though at the last minute I tried to stop it, I still felt like I killed my child. Growing up Catholic, I felt like I committed the worst sin in the world, to kill someone."

When Donna returned to her apartment, she felt completely alone with her loss, and she spent the next three weeks grieving off and on by herself in her bedroom. Then finally the phone rang. It was Scooter. "Why are you calling me?" Donna screamed.

"Well, I'm calling to see how you and the baby are doing," a repentant Scooter replied.

"I got rid of it. That's what you wanted, right?" Donna yelled angrily.

"I'm sorry, I didn't mean it. I didn't mean to hurt you." How could someone not mean to sexually assault another human being? It was insane. And yet those were the first words of comfort and understanding anyone had spoken to Donna since she lost her child, and his words felt so good that she craved more.

"Maybe we could heal together," Donna thought to herself. "Maybe we could lean on each other and comfort each other over the child we lost together. Plus, if I could just look in his eyes, I'd know if he truly cares about me," she hoped.

"Hey, Donna, why don't you come over so we can talk some more," suggested Scooter before they hung up.

A few days later Donna boarded the bus to Scooter's house, where he lived with his mother and older sister. When Donna arrived, Scooter opened his front door and escorted her up the stairs to his bedroom. As they sat on his bed, Donna began to talk about the child they had lost and how she wanted to stop the abortion at the last minute but couldn't, and now was feeling so much guilt and heartache for having gone against her Catholic faith. Tears rolled down her face. Scooter moved closer to Donna, holding her in his arms, and then, without warning, attempted to kiss her and slowly began removing her shirt. When Donna felt his hand pull at her bra, she couldn't believe what she was feeling and jumped off the bed as if hit by a bolt of lightning.

"I just lost a child, just killed a child! Do you know what the fuck I just did! Do you know what the fuck I just did! You better get off of me!" Donna screamed at the top of her lungs.

"I know, Donna, that's why I want to give you another child," responded Scooter.

Donna nearly fainted in anger. "This can't be happening to me. I have to be dreaming. There must be something wrong with this dude." She went out of her mind.

"Scooter! Scooter! Scoooooooter!" yelled Scooter's older sister from the bottom of the steps leading up to Scooter's bedroom. "Who you got in there? Who you got in Mama's house? You know you can't have no girls in here! You better get her outta here. You better get that bitch outta here before I kick her ass myself," Scooter's older sister screamed as she stood in nothing but a white bra and slip. Scooter quickly gathered Donna and rushed her down the stairs, racing passed his older sister, who took a swing at Donna's head and missed. Scooter then pushed Donna out the front door.

Donna stood on Scooter's porch crying, feeling sharp pains in her stomach from her recent abortion. "Scooter, I ain't going nowhere until you call me a cab," she hollered. "I'm not leaving this porch until you call me a cab."

"You blood clot, I will kick her ass," Scooter's older sister screamed from inside the doorway.

Donna quickly took her keys out of her pocket and put the sharpest one in between her fingers. "I'm going to rip her a new hole," she said to herself. "I'm going to cut her up and slice and dice her."

Finally the cab arrived. The driver jumped out of his taxi when he heard the screaming coming from inside the house. "What's wrong with her?" he asked Donna.

"She's crazy," Donna said, as she jumped in and slammed and locked the door, just in time for Scooter's sister to run outside in her bra and panties and start banging on the car. Meanwhile, Scooter remained in the doorway, "just standing here, looking like an idiot." The taxi finally pulled away, and Donna vowed never to see Scooter again. The one time he did call her a few days later, Donna picked up the phone and coolly told him to "lose my number."

Then, a year later, Scooter showed up at Donna's apartment out of the blue, drunk and stammering from the hallway. "You killed my baby! I can't have no kids anymore," he lamented. "You were the only one I had one with!"

When Donna heard that, she was so angry, she opened her apartment door and yelled, "I can't help it if your seeds are damaged. I can't help if your seeds ain't working no more. You need to stop smoking the ganja root," and slammed the door. That was the last she heard of Scooter.

CANCER

As a result of the Pap smear Donna received right after her abortion, she learned she had cervical cancer, following a trend among African Americans, who researchers believe have the highest rate of cancer-related deaths in the nation, in part, because of the multiple daily stressors of their environments.[1]

"You are fortunate we caught this so early," her doctor explained. "If not for your abortion, you wouldn't have known until it was much too late."

For the following two years, just before I was born in 1980, Donna was required to visit the hospital each month to have biopsy procedures performed on her cervix, the small, neck-like tissue that bridges the vagina and the uterus. Each time they checked, however, her doctors were unable to find the exact location of the cancerous cells, so they scheduled Donna to come back the following month, removing another piece of tissue from her body in a painful procedure that left scars. The two-year cycle of healing for three weeks and then having her scars reopened on the fourth week was almost unbearable. During this period Donna stopped having sex altogether, and her doctors pre-scribed birth control pills to be sure she wouldn't become pregnant. She lost hope that her cancer would ever be treated effectively.

Then one day a different doctor located the cancerous cells. He took a small tool that looked like a ballpoint pen with a round circle at the end and performed a procedure he called "freezing," in which he peeled a layer of skin from her cervix and removed the cancer. Then, to be sure he got it all, he took another biopsy, which showed Donna was cancer-free.

"Donna, I want to be frank with you. I'm glad that we caught this early, but you should know that the cancer will come back eventually," explained the doctor. "In twenty-five years, you are likely to have cancer again, so please get checked regularly."

"Sure enough," Donna said, "I did get breast cancer thirty years later. But what I discovered is that my body is not like other bodies. I also have horseshoe-shaped kidney, abnormally large pancreas ducts, a rare spinal problem called Chiara, asthma, gall-stones, and skin issues. The devil don't want me here, been using my body to take me out from the beginning."

SEXUAL ASSAULT

Donna did not have her second daughter, Joy, for another nine years, seven years after she aborted her son. However, she did begin to date again, hoping to find Mr. Right. Unfortu-nately, inviting men into her life only led to more violence, mental abuse, and sexual brutality. On one occasion in par-ticular, her boyfriend's brother attempted to rape Donna under the pretense of being concerned about her safe return home from a dance club.

"Donna, the club is closing. I'll give you a ride home," the brother suggested. The polite young man recognized Donna on the dance floor at the Rondevue in Roxbury and approached her as the club was shutting down for the night.

"No, that's okay. I'll walk home," Donna declined the offer. "It isn't too far."

"No, my brother would be mad if I didn't give you a ride," the young man insisted in a more aggressive yet still endearing tone.

"No! I'll walk home," Donna responded, holding her ground as she exited the club by herself and started walking down a well-lit street in the middle of Roxbury. A few minutes later, as she strolled toward her apartment, she noticed a vehicle crawling beside her.

"Donna, come on, get in," the young man insisted.

Donna turned to see his face peering through the car window. She hesitated for a moment, then agreed. "I said, 'Okay, what the heck,' and that was my worst mistake. I got in the car," she explained, still blaming herself all these years later for this young man's brutality.

Donna opened the passenger side door and sat down in the vehicle. Once she was inside, the young man struck up a polite conversation as Donna kept her eyes on the road to be sure he was headed toward her apartment, which was right down the street. As the young man neared Donna's front door, a feeling of relief washed over her body. Then he sped right past her entrance.

"What are you doing? My place is right there. Take me home!" she protested, but the young man shrugged off her words, telling her that his brother would be getting off work soon, and it would be nice of her to surprise him in the apartment the two brothers shared. At this point, Donna began to feel uncomfortable, her hands sweating, and she could only hope that her boyfriend would actually be in the apartment when the two of them arrived.

As soon as they pulled up, Donna saw that her boyfriend's bedroom window light was on. She hastily opened the passenger-side door, got out of the car, and bolted up the stairs leading to the bedroom, hoping to see her boyfriend inside. When she opened the door, however, she instead found three strangers having sex on the mattress.

"Wait a minute! Where is your brother at?" Donna turned to face her boyfriend's brother, who had been following close behind her the whole time.

"Oh, he'll be here soon. Let's go into the workout room and wait for him," he replied, before coaxing Donna into his bedroom and away from the moaning of the others.

"You have a very beautiful family," commented Donna, peering at his family photos, just as the lights flicked off and the two of them became enveloped in darkness.

"The lights went off!" yelled Donna. "What's going on? The lights are off." In the blindness of the dark, Donna felt a man's hands grab her body from behind and violently throw her down on the bed, the brother putting the full weight of his massive frame and chest on top of her.

"You're gonna be with me! You shoulda never been with my brother. It should have been me, not him. You're gonna give it to me," he shouted at Donna as he began to assault her.

"I never knew that he held anger for me because he couldn't have me," Donna recalled painfully through her tears.

The brother pulled down his pants and attempted to penetrate Donna with his penis. She thought to herself, "Not again." Donna grabbed his penis in her hands and "tried to break it off," just as she had done as a little girl in the Point with the other men who believed they were entitled to her body.

"Just give it up, Donna. Just give it up," he demanded.

"Alright," she responded. But then, "When he went to put it inside, I caught him off guard, and I got the best of him. I grabbed it and tried to break it. I fell off the bed, and I rolled onto the floor, and I felt my arm hit a chair and it was metal. It was pitch black. I got a hold of that chair and I started swinging it, just swinging in darkness. I was hitting him. I was literally hitting him; I was tearing him up with this chair. The next thing, I turn around, and he turned the light on, and he laughed at me. I said, 'You're taking me home. You're gonna take me home.' He said, 'Are you gonna tell my brother?' I said, 'If I tell your brother, he'll kill you. He will kill you for what you just did.'" Donna went home in tears.

JOY'S FATHER

A few years later Donna met Joy's father at the Unity Sportsmen and Culture Club, while listening and dancing to the catchy rhythms of Afro-Caribbean beats. Earlier that evening, her Aunt Charlotte had knocked on Donna's front door and begged Donna to join her at the club.

"Aunt Charlotte wanted to make her boyfriend jealous by going dancing that night," Donna remembered. "I was in my pajamas and really didn't want to go, but eventually I said yes." When the two women arrived at the club, they walked in proudly, wearing nice clothes and expensive makeup. They found chairs for themselves near the dance floor as Charlotte spotted her boyfriend in the distance and pretended to ignore him. Donna struck a pose of indifference, too, sitting with her legs crossed, a feigned look of boredom on her beautiful face.

"Hi," a sweet, baritone voice spoke to Aunt Charlotte from the dance floor and approached. "My name is DeAngelo. Will you dance with me?" Charlotte smiled. Her plan to rile her boy-friend was falling nicely into place. Extending her hand to DeAngelo, she sashayed onto the dance floor to the rhythm of the reggae beats and danced with him up close, the two smiling and chatting coolly while moving to the music. Once several songs were over, Charlotte took DeAngelo's hand and brought him over to her niece. "Donna, DeAngelo is so nice, and he's got a BMW, and he's an accountant, too. You should get to know him. DeAngelo, I want you to meet my niece, Donna." Donna rolled her eyes. She knew what her aunt was up to. Charlotte had used DeAngelo to make her boyfriend jealous, and now she was pawning the young man off on her.

DeAngelo stared into Donna's eyes. "Would you like to dance, Donna?" he asked in a smooth baritone. "Please, please," he begged her with a sexy smile.

"Ok, I'll dance with you," Donna relented. Once on the dance floor, the two moved together with an undeniable chemistry, their hips locking in a rhythmic wind. After each song, their bodies seemed to inch closer until, before they realized it, they were dancing cheek to cheek, swaying back and forth to a slow song, embracing each other's waists by the end of the night. Donna felt so good and comfortable in his arms. DeAngelo wasn't trying to rub on her, either. Instead, he held her with a gentleman's touch, his fingertips circling her waist softly as Car-lene Davis's sultry voice sang "Stealing Love on the Side." "Stealing love . . . / You held me in your arms and made love to me. / Fueled my heart's desire, / Your lips caressed me / Your body possessed me / Now I'd keep you if I could / If time would stand still and leave us two this way."[2]

DeAngelo and Donna got lost in time, so much so that when the music stopped and the club lights came on, they continued to dance. Suddenly Donna heard clapping sounds, breaking their lovers' trance, and looked around the club. Everyone had made a circle around the two and were clapping in admiration of their obvious connection. Donna and DeAngelo suddenly pulled back from each other in embarrassment and slowly walked back to her chair. "What was I thinking?" Donna thought to herself as she sat down. "Whooo damn! What just happened?" she whispered.

Suddenly Aunt Charlotte came running over. "Donna, the club is closing. Come on, we gotta go!" she said, as several young suitors who were not her boyfriend followed closely behind. Charlotte yanked Donna's hand before she could get a word out to DeAngelo, and the two women hotfooted it out of the dance hall, laughing the whole time. When they jumped into Charlotte's car, several handsome men, including DeAngelo, surrounded it, motioning for the women to roll down their windows and write down their phone numbers. Donna spotted DeAngelo and cracked her window slightly.

"Donna, can I call you sometime?" he asked with a smile.

"Yes, you can call me," she consented. DeAngelo anxiously searched for a piece of paper in his pocket. "Give me your hand," Donna motioned, as DeAngelo stuck his hand through the slight opening in the window. She gently held his fingers and wrote her digits on his soft skin.

DeAngelo smiled and joked, "I'm never going to wash my hand!"

That was March 20, the day before her nephew Timmy's birthday. On March 21 Donna went outdoor roller skating with her friends to celebrate Timmy's birthday near Fenway Park, the baseball stadium that has historically felt off limits to Boston's African American inner-city residents. By the time she returned home late that evening, Olivia was beside herself. "Donna, some boy named DeAngelo been calling all day! He left his number. Will you please call this boy back so he can stop calling my phone?!"

Donna returned DeAngelo's call, and their connection over the phone was as magnetic as it had been on the dance floor. They talked for hours, and DeAngelo was a good listener. He welcomed her insecurities. Even when she told him she had been mistreated and cheated on several times before and was afraid of giving her heart to another man, DeAngelo patiently countered with, "Just give me a chance."

On their first date, DeAngelo had a car accident, and Donna stayed late with him at the hospital.

"I love you, Donna," DeAngelo acknowledged after he had been discharged and they sat in his car. "I know you don't love me, but you will learn to love me. And you are going to be my wife and have my children," he promised. Those words hit Donna hard. She admired his bold courage and especially his composure when she didn't say "I love you" back on their first date.

DeAngelo was such a charmer. It was the first time any man had made Donna feel the pleasure of romance. When they went out to eat, he always pulled her chair out, waiting until she sat down to take his seat. If her silverware was stained, DeAngelo cleaned it before she ate. He opened and closed doors and brought her sweet-smelling flowers. One evening, when they argued at her mother's house, Donna told DeAngelo to leave. The next morning she found him asleep at Olivia's kitchen table.

"I can't leave you," he said when she woke him up. "I told you, I love you."

That was it. Donna made the decision to stop playing games with DeAngelo when she saw him drooling at their kitchen table. She would give her love to him, and she did, more deeply than to any man before, and for a while it was like heaven. They frequented movies and fancy dinners, and they drove his new Ford, where they had all-night conversations. Donna really loved the sound of DeAngelo's voice, and they shared the same tastes in music. She knew almost every song that played on the cassette player in his car, and they sang along: "Reasons, the reasons that we're here / The reasons that we fear / Our feelings won't disappear / And after the love game has been played / All our illusions were just a parade / And all the reasons start to fade / La, la la."[3] Or it was: "You're just too good to be true / I can't take my eyes off you / You'd be like heaven to touch / I wanna hold you so much / At long last love has arrived / And I thank God I'm alive / You're just too good to be true," Donna sang, looking into DeAngelo's beautiful brown eyes.[4] DeAngelo even took Donna and her daughter, Alexis, down to Franklin Park, where the three settled down on the grass for a picnic after a full day riding around to the soundwaves of Earth, Wind, and Fire, the Delfonics, and the Four Seasons.

But DeAngelo changed when Donna became pregnant with Joy. "He switched on me. But he loved me. I knew he loved me. He wanted to be the man that I wanted him to be, but he just could not be that person," Donna sighed. Instead of committing to Donna and their unborn child, DeAngelo cheated on Donna, even as he continued to sweep her off her feet. Donna felt so good in DeAngelo's presence that even when she discovered his infidelity, which opened up old emotional wounds, she felt powerless to leave, hoping to win back his affection by being a better girlfriend. And the few times she did summon up the courage to resist DeAngelo's advances for sex because she felt betrayed, he became abusive with his words, suggesting that Donna was worthless without him. And Donna believed him. It was one of the reasons she had his child and stayed with DeAngelo for the next seven years, knowing he was sexing other women, yet she remained by his side.

"I was with him for seven years. The man never laid a hand on me. The man never touched me. But I got mental abuse, and mental abuse is worse than physical, because at least when you have physical abuse, there are scars, and they heal, but the mental abuse stays with you forever. And then when I tried to leave him, he threatened me. And I kept staying with him. He cheated on me with one woman, and that one right there was okay, but when it went from one to two to three to four to five, I didn't care. You can do whatever you want to do. We were together for seven years, and one of them years, I did not have sex with him for six months. I insisted that he use a condom, cuz I didn't trust him. I didn't trust him. When I wanted to leave him, and he finally knew I wanted to leave him, he seen I was slipping away from him, and he kept thinking it was another man. I said, 'That's what you want to think, honey. But I want you to know, I'm leaving you because you're not the man you claim to be any more.' But I stayed with him for seven years."

After Donna had Joy, she caught DeAngelo cheating on her several more times before she finally decided to leave. "One time, he told me that he needed to run to the store down the street from my house. I look out the window, and I see his car in bumper-to-bumper traffic. I'm like, 'Where is he going? You told me you were going to the store, right? So why is your car in traffic?' Snooky! He done it again! I didn't even put my sneakers on. I ran out there in the snow."

There was Donna, running in her white socks down the snowy pavement, right into standstill traffic, angered by her boyfriend.

When she went to bang on his car window, though, she realized he wasn't even in the vehicle. "There's this chick driving the car. I go [knocking sound]; I said, 'Where's DeAngelo?'"

"Oh, he went to bring his niece home," the young woman replied.

"I said, 'His niece?'"

"Yeah, she lives down in that building," the woman said, as she pointed to Donna's apartment.

"I said, 'Okay, can I speak to you for a minute?' Before she said no, I opened that car door so quick. She tried to stop me. I popped right in that car. I said, 'Go up the street and pull it over to the side.'"

On the side of the icy road, Donna stared into the young woman's bewildered face.

"Who's DeAngelo's niece?" Donna asked, like a teacher giving her worst student a pop quiz.

"She's the little girl he just brought inside the building," she answered.

"That little girl is our daughter, and I've been with DeAngelo for five years now!" boomed Donna.

"No, you're not. That's not his kid; he doesn't have no kids," the shocked young woman pleaded.

"Yes, she is. She looks exactly like him. I've been with him for five years," said Donna, as the lady broke down in tears, confiding in Donna that she had been with DeAngelo for five months, and he had beaten her up on several occasions. "She's telling me how he beats on her, hit her in the head. She said, 'Does he beat you?' When she said that, I think I blacked out for a second. I said, 'Do we have earthquakes in Massachusetts?' I think I literally blacked out. I said, 'Are you serious? That man ain't that doggone crazy! Put his hands on me? Oh, no.' I was heated. I was in there looking for something to jack that car up.

I was like—'I just want to cut it up. Why can't I have something in my hand?' I was about to tear the seats up, everything. She's like, 'No, no! Don't mess up his car!' I was [shooting noise]. I said, 'Honey, I don't think you want to stop me.' She backed her hands up like this. But that's when I backed down. I said come in my house. I said, 'First of all, let me be very clear. I have no beef with you because you have no knowledge of me; I have no knowledge of you. I have no beef with you.'"

Once Donna escorted the young woman into her apartment, she went back downstairs to hunt for DeAngelo. As soon as she spotted him across the street, he booked it into a nearby video store where Donna knew the owner. "He knew his goose was cooked," she said. Donna walked defiantly into the video store, planning to yank each video off the shelf to get to DeAngelo's hide. To Donna's pleasure, a young clerk pointed to a door in the back of the store. As she moved toward it, the owner stopped her.

"Donna, you don't want to do it," he said calmly. "Donna, he's not worth it, and you're better than that." Donna looked at the owner, thought for a moment about his words, and then relented, not because she felt she was above cleaning DeAngelo's clock, but because she didn't want to disrespect the owner's store.

But she left him with these words: "You tell him when he comes outside, I'll be waiting for him. He's gonna have to deal with me. He's gonna have to face me."

Donna stormed out of the store, crossed the snow-filled street, and stomped up the stairs to her apartment, where she perched herself on the windowsill overlooking the entrance of the video store. "We are going to wait for him together," Donna said decidedly to DeAngelo's girlfriend, who smartly pulled up a chair next to her. As the two women waited, they exchanged stories about their relationship with DeAngelo, most of which left his new girlfriend in a state of shock.

"She can't believe it, but I'm not shocked," said Donna. "She's more in shock than I am. I'm just getting angrier by the minute. I just want to jack him up. Let's be real. I just want to tear him to shreds like a paper shredder."

As Donna's emotions boiled over, there was DeAngelo, suddenly tiptoeing out of the video store.

"There he goes right there!" screamed Donna.

All 6'3" of DeAngelo's black body gingerly tiptoed across the packed white snow and bolted toward a nearby running car with several men inside. As DeAngelo attempted to squeeze himself into the backseat, Donna raced down the stairs, this time with her shoes on and his girlfriend following close behind. She made a beeline straight for DeAngelo, while his girlfriend bolted for his new Volvo, which she had parked on the side of the frosty road. When DeAngelo realized he wasn't going to get away before Donna got to him, he slipped out of the car and hauled it toward his Volvo, Donna fast on his heels. As he neared, DeAngelo yelled to his girlfriend, "I don't know that woman! She's crazy!" just before jumping into the passenger seat. "Oh, you don't know me?" screamed Donna, pointing her finger through a crack in the passenger-side window, almost poking out his eyeball. "I let him get in the car—and when I say I let him, I let him—he gets in the car, and then I go over to the car, and they had the window cracked so that just my finger could go in," laughed Donna. "I said, 'You see that child in the window right there you said is your niece? You won't see her no more.' He said, 'Donna, I'm sorry, I love you,'" as his girlfriend sped off and down the wintery Boston street.

Soon after, Donna received a phone call from another young woman. On the other end of the line, one of DeAngelo's other girlfriends began spitting rap lyrics like she was a battle rapper, turning the letters of Donna's name into a diss track: "D is for . . . O is for. . . ."

"She told me when I kiss his lips, bleep, bleep, bleep. I was hysterical. My younger sister, she was good at rapping. She got on that phone, and she out-rapped that girl. Do you hear me? My sister literally out-rapped her. At this point, I am like a raging volcano." As Donna's sister and the young woman battle-rapped, DeAngelo happened to walk through the door. Donna went ballistic. "I hand my daughter to my relative, and I picked up this lead pipe, and I'm just swinging to hit him. I wanted to kill him. It would've been just as easy as pie. Took the ring off [of their recent engagement] and threw it at him. He didn't care, either. I don't think he picked the ring up. Then he picked the pipe up, and my sister was screaming in the window. He picked the pipe up, and by the grace of God, when he went to swing and hit me, I ducked. When I ducked, I felt the breeze go right over my head. When he realized that he was gonna hurt me, he dropped the pipe and ran. I chased him all the way down the street to Columbus Ave." The mental abuse Donna experienced with DeAngelo had now escalated to physical violence.

Donna was at the end of her rope. The pain of loving DeAngelo, only for him to cheat on her and then for her to allow him back into her life so he could do it all over again had wrecked her nerves and self-esteem. She was a "raging volcano" inside, and her emotional fire was so intense that she began to have suicidal thoughts again. "I was trying to give this man a chance and to do right by us and his daughter. That was the Lord in me. But he had that wickedness in him that he just couldn't let go. And I can't live like that. And at times, when I was with him, I felt like I wanted to kill myself more than two or three times. No, this relationship had to be over."

The day that Donna decided to leave DeAngelo, she was sitting on a kitchen chair in her bedroom, "looking out the window, and I was shaking so bad my nerves were just shot." DeAngelo entered the room, got on his knees, and recited the lines that before had always returned her to being his emotional servant.

"I never meant to hurt you. You're my first love. I want to marry you. Please give me a chance."

But Donna had finally made up her mind to say no. "I can't," she said. "Every time you walk out that door, you take a piece of me with you. You walk out, you're happy. I'm not happy. I'm miserable. I do everything for you. I did things for you that I shouldn't have done for you, but I did. And you took advantage of me. You took my niceness for weakness. You thought I was naïve. You thought I was gullible. You thought I was easy game to play. But I still have my dignity intact. My family, everybody knows how you cheat on me. And you dishonor me, you disgrace me every time you do that. And everyone knows. Just because you got a job and make money, I should stay with you? You can't buy my love, cuz it wasn't money that I fell in love with. I fell in love with you. I don't want to be with you no more. You are not the man you claim to be. And I want you to remember that, to know we're not together because of you," she said.

When DeAngelo recognized the look of conviction in Donna's eyes, he grew silent, stood up, and walked out of the room. A few days later, DeAngelo called Donna on the telephone.

"Donna," he said, "if you ever need me, I'll always be there for you."

"Don't sit around waiting for it cuz you won't get no call from me," Donna responded, permanently ending the relationship with her second daughter's father by the time she was thirty-two years old.

"I THOUGHT I WOULD DIE
OF LONELINESS"

Donna fell in love with a man for the final time when she was forty-three. She met Junior on the dance floor at a Cape Verdean nightclub off of Columbia Road. Junior was twenty-eight years old. "I was attracted to young guys and they were attracted to me. At forty-five, I looked like I was thirty-five," explained Donna. "For some reason, everybody that was coming towards me was younger. I'm not saying I'm all that, but I don't know, for some reason, the enemy would have men view me as a sex symbol," she revealed.

"And I was not what they were seeing on the outside. That's not who I am on the inside. One time, this man followed me into a children's store," Donna remembered, recalling one particularly disturbing encounter with sexual harassment. "He said, 'I never did this before, but I just gotta have your number.' One time, a guy almost crashed into a wall. I was much smaller than I am now, and I had a shape and everything. But I said, 'No, don't look at my body. Look at my face, who I am on the inside.'"

As Donna danced the night away to Zuka music, Cape Verdean men watched her hips sway to the thump of rhythmic beats, until Junior finally found the courage to introduce himself. It wasn't the first time Junior had watched her from afar. He noticed her on several different nights, but she was so much older than he was, and he was afraid to approach her.

"I said to him, 'I'm too old to be with you,' but it didn't matter." Within days, Donna and Junior were going on romantic dates, spending time in Donna's apartment, enjoying each other's conversation and having passionate sex.

Donna was in love and happier than she had been in a long time. Then one evening early in their relationship, Junior didn't show up for their date and didn't call for several days. Donna was confused and hurt but wanted to give him a chance to explain himself, so she waited before passing judgment. A few days later he showed up at the apartment door unannounced, walked into the kitchen, and begged her to forgive him. Donna looked into his beautiful brown eyes and forgave. But in that moment she knew deep down that "their relationship began to change. That's the day that he started drifting from me."

Junior was cheating on Donna. She couldn't deny it when he came down with a case of chlamydia. Yet even then she chose to stay by his side, justifying her decision by forcing him to wear protection during sex. And before she knew it, she was descending down the same spiral of unhappiness again, placing her trust and self-worth in an undeserving man.

"I kept saying to him, if you don't want to be with me, just let me know. I'll go on and live my life. I've never been that type of person that runs behind a man. But he kept always coming back to me. When I said, 'Listen, leave me alone, stay away from me,' he kept coming back to me, saying I'm sorry. And I fell for the lie. It was a lie. I was falling for the lie."

By the time Donna realized her relationship with Junior was toxic, it was too late. He had taken possession of her, and she had already "entered a deep state of depression," unable to resist his advances during his sporadic visits. "He kept coming around me, calling me, showing up at my house. Just basically tormenting me. The enemy had him tormenting me. I kept telling him to stay away; he wouldn't stay away. He wasn't really stalking me. He just wouldn't leave me alone. And then when he came around me, I gave in to him. And then every time he walked out that door, he took me with him." Donna lived for his attention. "I lost weight. I lost thirty-five to forty pounds. I got dehydrated. He would leave, and I would see him maybe two, three months later. This cycle went on. It got to the point where I thought all I was good for was sex."

Junior's disregard for Donna's feelings and her toxic need for his attention destroyed her physical health and frayed her relationship with her children. "And the last time it happened, I was sitting, I would get a cup, smaller than this, probably that much, and I would have ginger ale, and I would just take maybe two or three sips in one day. And remember, there's twenty-four hours in a day. And I took two or three sips. Not being aware that I was slowly making myself sick. My mom was crying. My kids were crying to my mother. They were saying, 'Nana, please talk to my mother, please.' They hated him. My oldest daughter wanted to do something to him. My youngest daughter was going to college, coming out of high school at the time. I was just so depressed. When I went to do things with her for her prom dress, I wasn't motivated. I was just there but not there. My oldest daughter had to do the things that I should have did, but I was so depressed. And I hated myself for being that way. To this day, I'm ashamed. And there's times that I think about it, and my kids forgive me, but to think that I got that low."

"THE BATTLE'S NOT YOURS, IT'S THE LORD'S"

Donna began to cry painfully as we spoke on her couch about the lowest moment in her life. "So, at this point with this guy, I was just broken from all the broken relationships, and this was the end of it. I couldn't take no more. I couldn't deal with no more. I was hurting so bad, giving my all, loving this man, giving him everything, helping him. Not judging him when he had a disease, and I was hurt. And I laid in my bed in my bedroom, and I looked up at the wall, and I said, 'Lord, I've got to do something.' When I was in the hospital, the doctor told me if I didn't do nothing, I was gonna die of loneliness. I never knew you could die of loneliness. And they said, I was gonna die of loneliness. I wasn't wanting him back. I just wanted him to leave me alone, just stay away from me. Just let me heal, and the enemy wouldn't let him leave me alone. He just come at me, kept coming and coming and coming. And I couldn't take it anymore. The enemy put the idea in me, 'Well, kill yourself. If you're not here, he won't bother you.'"

As Donna lay in bed staring at the ceiling, contemplating suicide, she remembered one final option. "I said, 'God, I'm doing everything, but I haven't called on you.' I said, 'God, I haven't called on your Holy Spirit. I need help; please help me.' I said, 'I can't leave. I can't leave my kids. I can't leave my grandkids. My daughters need me.' My oldest daughter's father wasn't really there for her when she grew up, it was just me and her. And then I had my youngest one nine years later. And my kids are my whole—I'm their world. I'm all they have, even though my youngest daughter's father is in her life. But I am mommy, and there is no one like your mommy, and I couldn't hurt my kids. I couldn't hurt 'em. I could not put this on them. I couldn't put it on them. I had to do something. They had already been through so much already. They couldn't have no more than that. I didn't know how I was gonna do it, but I had to do something."

That's when Donna's sister entered her bedroom. "She opened my door. I was so depressed that I would stay in my bedroom with my door closed in my house, and she came in the room, and usually I would yell at her to close the door. It was so bad, my youngest daughter wrote me a poem about me as a superwoman. She saw me lying in that bed every morning, depressed. I woke up that morning, and she had the letter on my blanket. That was it. That was it. I was not gonna let them take me from my kids," Donna sobbed as she spoke. "That was it. No, no, no, no. That was it for me. My sister came in that room, and I got up, and I heard this song in my mind from Yolanda Adams playing: 'There is no pain, Jesus can't feel/No hurt He cannot heal/For all things work according to His perfect will. . . . For the battle is not yours, it's the Lord's."5

Donna stood up from her bed and walked to her doorway. "I stepped out of my room, and I had to hear the rest of the song playing. I heard it, and I heard her saying, 'Hold your head up high. The battle's not yours, it's the Lord's.' Just that phrase, 'the battle's not yours.' It's like it's not my battle, I don't have to fight it. It's His battle. Just that little wisdom I received. I opened the door, and I said to my sister, 'Maya, can I go to church with you?' She said, 'Sure. The doors of the church are always open.'"

MORNING STAR BAPTIST CHURCH

Donna turned around and went back to her bedroom to get dressed. "I pulled on my stockings; I got runs in 'em. I said, 'I don't care; I'm going.' I go in my closet. I don't know what I want to wear. I felt like—'cause I was raised Catholic—you got to be presentable when you come to church," Donna explained, observing the strict liturgy of Catholic worship services. "I said, 'I don't care if I go in there with mismatched clothes. I'm getting outta here, the whole time, the whole time I was in the shower, I was crying. Oh, it hurt so bad. [Donna begins to sob again.] I hurt so bad. I was sitting there, and the water was pouring on me, and I was crying. The whole time, I truly believe Jesus was holding me the whole time. He was lifting me up. I was just the whole time crying. I got out of that tub, I got dressed, and I got in the car. And I'm still crying. I'm crying so much I can't stop. My sister's holding my hand. She's saying to me, 'Donna, it's gonna be alright.' I'm driving up Blue Hill Ave, and I'm still crying, I just can't stop crying. But not one time did I say take me home. Not one time did I say that. And we got in that church, the congregation was so nice. They said, 'Good morning, sister, bless you, sister.' That's what I heard. Then I sat down in the back of the church. This was an old church. The building used to be the old Church's Chicken Restaurant [in Roxbury]. The next thing, you turn around, I'm in the back of the church, and the choir was awesome! It's like listening to Kirk Franklin. Now in Catholic churches, we don't shout hallelujah. All of a sudden, I hear people shouting, 'Hallelujah, thank you Jesus, praise the Lord!' That's all I hear. 'Thank you, Lord. Hallelujah, Jesus, thank you.' This is all new to me. It's all new to me."

"IF THAT MAN AIN'T TREATING YOU NO GOOD, KICK HIM TO THE CURB!"

The jubilant sounds of the Black gospel choir, the ecstatic shouts of joy erupting spontaneously from Black congregants' sanctified mouths, and the welcoming gestures of the graceful ushers enclosed Donna in a sensual space of resistance to the hardness of life in the streets of Roxbury. In this new space of worship, she felt her black body had come home. She couldn't believe that Christians were allowed to incarnate the Holy Spirit in such a full-bodied, celebratory way. She bowed her head in the pews just as the magnanimous Black bishop John Borders III, the senior pastor, walked into the pulpit to deliver his sermon. Turning his body into "God's trombone,"[6] his voice quivered with life force, giving breadth to an impassioned urban feminist homily on the moral rightness of divorce in cases of emotional or physical domestic abuse, an idea that would have been heretical in the Catholic household of Donna's upbringing.

"I've got my head down. I don't look up, but I just hear him. I'm still depressed. All of a sudden, I hear him say, and these are his exact words: 'If that woman ain't treating you no good, kick her to the curb.' Now, Catholic religion, that's unorthodox to hear something like that. That got my eye, so when I heard that, I was like, hold up. 'Kick her to the curb'—that's something that you say in the street. I heard him say that. He said, 'If that man ain't treating you no good, kick him to the curb. If you've done all that you can, then they don't deserve you.' Then I heard him say, 'Did you stop to think, to see if he's worthy of you?' Made me question me! I questioned me!" Donna exclaimed, surprised by the first time that she challenged gendered constructions of herself and the world.

"That's when I looked up. It was like the Holy Spirit was talking through him to talk to me," effused Donna, mirroring the sentiments of the great German theologian Fredrich Schleiermacher, who understood preaching as an "incarnational event," in which the preacher's words become a vehicle for the presence of Christ in the listener by way of the sermon.[7] Donna's identity was beginning to shift from an object of her environment to a subject of something deeper within.

"That's all I needed to hear, 'cause God knows if I heard that, I was gonna snap out of it," exclaimed Donna. "The next thing you turn around, all of a sudden, I feel some hands behind my back, and I jump, 'Hallelujah!' And me, as I said, I'm Catholic when I'm walking in," Donna repeated, emphasizing how much she appreciated this new, embodied, spirit-centered religion of the Black church. "I'm looking around, who's looking at me? I felt so good!"

When Donna finally stepped out of Morning Star, she felt that "the joy of the Lord was with me. I walked out. I felt good," she smiled. Before that Sunday morning, Donna explained, "when I was so depressed, I let my house go. My house wasn't clean. I kept the kitchen clean and the bathroom clean, but I let the floor go. I didn't mop my floor. My grands would come in, and they would say, Nana, you ain't cleaned your floor. They could just come in and say my walls were black. My granddaughter, Amber, who is spiritually gifted like me, would see in the spirit world that my walls were black. She told my daughter that she didn't want to go and see me because my walls were black. So [on that Sunday morning after church], I opened up my windows. I pulled the shades, the venetian blinds up. I made me a dinner. I took my stereo system speaker and put it in the hallway and played gospel music, and it was blasting through the whole house, and I mopped my floors, twice, to make them brand new again."

And as Donna finished mopping her floors, suddenly the doorbell rang. It was Junior. Donna froze. "Wait a minute, I only got one service at the church. Why now? Lord have mercy, 'cause I ain't ready for this fool," she cried.

Donna pressed her back up against the door and closed her eyes to make Junior disappear. That's when, for the second time in her life, she heard the voice of an unseen presence.

"Open the door!" it said.

Donna looked around her apartment, but she was sure she was alone.

"Who said that?" she asked.

"Open the door!" the presence insisted. This time, Donna realized the voice was nonhuman, coming from no place in particular. She tried to ignore it, refusing to open her apartment door. "Open the door!" the voice commanded a third time.

"I said, 'Okay, then. I don't know who you are, but okay. I'm gonna follow your lead.' That's what I said within myself. 'Okay, I don't know who you are.' So I opened my front door."

When the door opened, Junior glided through graciously with a bed of long-stemmed red roses on his breast. He turned to Donna with a big, white-toothed smile and handed her the roses gently, before planting a juicy kiss on her cheeks.

"My hand was heavy," Donna acknowledged. Suddenly and unsure why, she felt emboldened. "Sit down," she commanded, surprising herself by the new tone of confidence and power in her voice. Junior seemed stunned by the backbone in her words. He took a seat on one of the twin couches, and Donna sat on the other. She stared at Junior, stone-faced, trying to mask the separate conversation taking place in her head. "What am I supposed to do now?" she asked herself. Just then, Junior launched into his soliloquy, apologizing, proclaiming his deep love for Donna and how, if she took him back, this time it would be different.

"Please forgive me," he said, his poise laced with a tinge of arrogance. "Wait for me for two more years. I'm working on getting my green card and getting settled so we can be together."

Junior slowly stood up, his eyes locked on Donna's, and walked over to her, trying to caress her with his strong hands.

"No, don't touch me. Don't touch me!" Donna said defiantly, before he could set a finger on her. Then she heard the nonhuman voice in her head again.

"Speak, my child," it enjoined.

"I opened up my mouth, and what came out of my mouth totally shocked me, 'cause I literally said to him, 'I want to thank you for what you did to me.' He looked at me like I had three heads!" It was the first time Donna had incarnated the Holy Spirit to speak prophetically to power.

Then Donna stood up and walked over to Junior, taking his hand in her firm grip and shaking it vigorously like a boss congratulating one of her lower employees.

"I want to thank you because what you did is gonna bring me to Jesus," she repeated, as Junior caught his mouth open. "And I put the law down, the law, not my law, Jesus's law," Donna expressed with conviction. "Don't call me. Don't come over my house. I said, 'Do not call me, do not come over my house. You call me, I'm gonna hang up on you. You come over my house, I'm gonna call the cops,' and I was not playing. I said, 'Satan brought you in my life to destroy it. But God used you to bring me to Him. You will not walk through these doors ever, ever again.' And to this day, that man ain't walked in my house, and I ain't seen him since. Hallelujah! Now you can't tell me my God ain't powerful! Hallelujah! I ain't seen him since. I have not seen that man since. Do you understand me? God kept him away. Sixteen years, I ain't seen that man in my house!" Donna celebrated her self-empowerment.

"My mother always said to me, you're gonna love someone that much, the only one you love that much is Jesus, cuz he will love you, he will not forsake you, he will not hurt you. So if you want to give all that love to someone, you give it to Jesus. So that, then and there, I took my mother's wisdom, and I gave it to Jesus. And at that moment, yeah, I was down with G.O.D., and Jesus was my man. And anytime someone came to me asking, 'Who you with?' or, 'Are you in a relationship?' I said, 'Yes, I do.' 'Well,

who is he?' they would ask. I said, 'Jesus. Whoop, can't go there!'
'Who's your man?' I said, 'G.O.D.' Who's 'G' 'O' 'D'?' they asked.
'God! Whoop, can't go there.' And that's the story of how I came
into God. That's where my journey started. That's what brung
me to where I am today."

II

METAMORPHOSIS

5

INCUBUS

At forty-six years old, Donna had discovered a new, embodied, spirit-centered religion of the Black church and began to experience her body as a "potential host of divine power," a vehicle for what Womanist scholar Dianne Stewart refers to as "recurring incarnation." After all, before he died, hadn't Jesus come through a woman's body, namely, Mary's?[1] Donna's lived spirituality did not emphasize suffering and death at the hands of powerful men as a Christian virtue. Rather, for her, incarnation was a life-giving event, the birth of a new consciousness, so to speak, which had empowered her to kick Junior to the curb.

But incarnation was a recurring process, and Donna's transformation was far from complete. Her most immediate concern was what do about sex now that Jesus was her "man." Although she did not accept traditional notions of Christian dualism, in which spirit is good and body is bad, Donna did begin to prioritize and to experience a higher regard for her inner life. So to protect the sanctity of her heart, she decided to give up sex with the men "of this world" altogether, and to solidify her spiritual union with Jesus.

At the same time, Junior and his new wife, Karla, didn't make Donna's commitment to abstinence any easier. A year after successfully removing Junior from her life, Donna received a phone call.

"Excuse me, but did my husband, Junior, call this number recently?" the woman queried Donna sharply. "Your phone number shows on his phone caller ID. Do you know my husband, Junior?"

"Sorry, you have the wrong number," Donna replied and quickly hung up the phone. Junior had been calling Donna, although each time she spotted his number, she refused to pick up. Instead, she turned to her Bible and reread her favorite passages, the ones she learned on Sundays, while faithfully attending Morning Star Baptist Church.

Another month went by before Karla called again.

"I told you, you have the wrong number," Donna insisted.

"Then why does my husband keep calling you?" asked Karla.

"I don't know, but you have the wrong number," Donna repeated before hanging up. A month later, Donna's phone rang again. It was Junior. She stared at the caller ID and let the call go to voicemail. A few moments later, the phone rang again. It was Karla, and she had caught Junior in the act. Donna picked up the phone.

"Don't you know that you are fooling around with a married man?" screamed Karla, as she wept on the other end of the line, her infant child crying along with her in the background.

"Listen," Donna said calmly, her heart broken. "I didn't want to, but I have to tell you the truth. Yes, I do know Junior, and I was with Junior before he knew you. You were able to give him a green card and that's why he married you. I've given my life to Jesus Christ, and I honor God's law, and I honor the sanctity of marriage. Junior has called, but I have not picked up the phone," she said.

Karla began sobbing. "I know he's been cheating on me," she confided in Donna. "Even when we first met, he had chlamydia."

"Honey, he had chlamydia when I first met him, too," Donna quipped. "We had already been together for two months at the time."

"I don't know what to do," lamented Karla. "My family even prayed over Junior and laid hands on him to change. If Junior calls again, can you let me know?" she begged.

"Yes, I will let you know," Donna agreed, before hanging up the phone.

Junior called Donna's number a few days later. This time, she decided to pick up the phone. "You are wrong the way you are treating her!" she scolded him. "She has your son. I am not giving you my time anymore!" Junior's voice brought back a flood of old feelings and insecurities.

Donna didn't want to be with him or any other man anymore. She was sure of it. Not with the kind of abuse women like Karla were going through every day. Donna hung up the phone in tears and began pleading with God to give her the strength not to feel any attraction toward them. She hurried to her daughter's bedroom, where she kept her stereo, and clicked on some gospel music to get closer to God. And that's when she remembered.

She had a flashback of Junior. She could feel his muscular body, his mouth whispering in her ear as her head lay on his naked chest, the two of them swaying back and forth to love songs. Donna felt the tingling of sexual desire, and she lost herself in the memory of being aroused with Junior years ago as they danced in their daughter's bedroom.

"God!" she screamed at the top of her voice. "I don't want to! You will never have me again. NoooooooooOOO! Never!" Donna fell to her knees, her forehead pressed against the floor as tears flowed down her cheeks. "I don't want to do this anymore. I don't want to be with a man anymore. I'm not going with them anymore. I don't want them in my house anymore," she begged God.

Yet despite her efforts, men continued to pursue Donna, and she remained attracted to them. Old boyfriends called her phone with the intention of hooking up, and new men, some of whom she tried to help with their personal problems as a good Christian friend, though they wanted more. One evening, one handsome brother pulled Donna aside and asked, looking deep into her eyes, "Can I take you out to dinner?"

Donna thought about it only long enough to reject his advances. "I made a covenant with God, and I'm not going to break it," she revealed with brutal honesty. "I don't have any physical feeling for you. Sleeping with you is condemning my life. You want me to break my promise to God. I'm not part of this package. We are just friends."

And Donna noticed that the more she put some distance between her body and those of these men, the clearer it became that all they wanted was, "sex, sex, sex, and sex." If at first she thought they were attracted to her beauty, the wool had now been snatched away from her eyes. "It was lust," she realized. "It was always lust. It's why, over the years, I was so self-conscious. It's why I loved the winter, when I could cover my butt with bulky clothes. When it wasn't winter, guys would always be like, 'Damn baby!' and I hated that reaction. And I got to the point that I tired of having sex. Sex was no longer love. It was lust. And it became like a job to me."

There were even times when guys approached Donna and asked her if she was on a sex vacation, and if so, would she be accepting applications or placing names on a wait-list. Men were obsessed with her physical appearance. "Every last of them were a bunch of freaks," she realized. And for the longest time, she was trying to make them happy at the expense of her own needs. "I had it in my mind that I'm not educated. I don't have a GED, and I don't have a master's, a bachelor's. But hey, I can be good at this, at sex. I used to watch porno movies when my children were gone out of the house to learn things to please men. And the men in my life were okay with this, but I was never okay with it. It was the only thing I thought I was good at. I was living a lie. I was doing all this for them and wasn't getting nothing in return."

REGENERATION: THE FIRST BLESSING

Donna continued to attend Morning Star Baptist Church regularly, "to get to know Jesus," as she put it, even though she didn't quite know how. After a while her sister stopped bringing her to the church building on Blue Hill Avenue, so she made her way there on her own, making sure to get there by ten o'clock for the eleven o'clock service, because by 10:15 the sanctuary would be jam-packed with Black congregants preparing for worship. Donna didn't mind where she sat during the service, but if she could get there early, her favorite spot was in the fourth pew back from the pulpit, seated right on the end closest to the aisle. From there she enjoyed a direct line of sight to Bishop Borders, so that when he spoke, she could receive the Word. Sometimes, the bishop's voice would get so intense and rhythmic that Donna would suddenly "catch the Holy ghost" right there in the pews while the bishop sang his sermon. Moving away, slightly, from her Catholic roots, Donna's became a spirit-centered faith, and she especially loved the way Bishop Borders based his teachings on the Bible. When he preached, she could "feel the Word of God from his teachings" and often scribbled notes to meditate over his sermons and read the scriptures he cited at home. To learn more about Jesus, Donna also asked her daughter Joy's Jamaican grandmother, whom Donna admired as a holy woman, which passages in the Bible she should read.

"Go all the way from Romans to the book of Revelations," the woman advised, and that's just what Donna did, doing her best to read the scriptures at her kitchen table, while listening to Yolanda Adams on her cassette player and cooking savory Southern meals. Donna even caught the Holy Spirit once in her kitchen during a Yolanda Adams song, crying out to God for the strength to let Junior and other men like him remain in her past.

"I'm not going back there!" she affirmed.

Donna was prepared to renounce her body's habit of desiring men. She had just returned to her Roxbury apartment from Morning Star one Sunday. She felt tired and eventually laid down on her mattress and fell asleep. While lying on the bed, she had a vivid dream, in which she felt led by the presence of the Holy Spirit.

"The Holy Spirit had me go through all the men that I had lived with, fell in love with, that broke my heart," she explained. Donna awoke the next morning with almost visceral pain and tears running down her soft cheeks. She vaulted off the bed enraged and punched the wall with her fists.

"Why, Lord, why? I don't want to feel this. Let it out. Let it out. Let it out!" she cried. "The Holy Spirit was telling me let it go. You're holding on to this. You need to let this go so I can come in," explained Donna, describing a process some Christian traditions refer to as a regeneration, or "first blessing," in which an individual is birthed into new life by the Holy Spirit. As one theologian put it: "We are accustomed to think and speak of the grace of pardon and regeneration as the first blessing: and it was the first blessing which effected an inward moral change in our heart life, and in our attitude and relationship toward God. . . . Regeneration was not only a blessing, but a work of grace divinely inwrought, changing our very nature, and bringing us into the glorious relationship of children, making us sons of God. . . . The first [blessing] is the birth of the Spirit, in which he receives spiritual life."[2]

By surfacing the pain of her trauma with men, Donna believed that the Holy Spirit was building a pristine altar for itself within her consciousness, birthing her into a new awareness of her value. "I was keeping it to myself. Whenever I spoke about 'em [men], I was mad, I was angry. The Holy Spirit knew I wasn't at peace. I stayed in my room for almost a weekend crying. He wanted me to express all that hurt, to pour it all out of me. And then, after I let it out, on the last day, it got calm."

This was a stunning reversal for a woman in her mid-forties living in the projects of inner-city Boston, who had survived multiple sexual assaults and attempted suicides, and who only had an eighth-grade education. But Donna's increased sense of self-worth was not being derived from book knowledge. This was an embodied way of knowing, an inner divine consciousness, which did not require empirical evidence or external validation. Hers was a lived religion derived from the "recurring incarnation" of the Holy Spirit.

The Holy Spirit worked on Donna from the inside out over the next few days until her rage subsided and her head became cool. And as she sat on the edge of her bed, Donna reaffirmed her covenant with Jesus. Like the Catholic nuns whom she aspired to be as a girl but had been made to feel too dirty to emulate, she chose never be involved in a romantic relationship with a man again for the rest of her life. When she really thought about it, most men she crossed paths with were socially conditioned to view her as sexual property anyway. "My relationships that I had with men, it wasn't because of my face, it was because of the intimacy. Their love for me was very, very strong. But their pants were weaker. They were much weaker. I realized that in order for a man to be in my life, that he had to be able to stand the test of the devil, of Satan."

THE SPIRIT OF LUST

"You got more time on you?" Donna asked me quietly as we settled on her beige couch and she prepared to tell me something that she felt I might not be able to comprehend. A few nights after the Holy Spirit had chosen to indwell in her body and to "make her a new mind," she went to bed and, to her surprise, "woke up" in another world, one she would later refer to as the "spirit world."

The first time she entered that world she was confused. She noticed that the spirit world looked just like the physical world, except it operated under different rules. For instance, in the spirit world, although her bedroom appeared a little darker than usual, it was basically the same. Her full-sized mattress still sat right in the middle of the room, and next to that, her wooden dresser with a mirror settled up against the left wall, and above that, her venetian blinds fluttering as they always did, gently in the breeze. And just like in the physical world, she possessed a body, but it was lighter and more ephemeral. She could still walk around her small apartment with legs and use hands to open doors and turn on lights or grab the remote to watch television, but she could also do things that didn't make much sense. For one, she could fly, or at least float in midair. And even when she walked, it was more like gliding as she moved across her carpet, like she was roaming with spiritual feet.

The spirit world was also full of sinister things. For example, on that first night, when she opened her intangible eyes, Donna saw a charcoal-black man with horns staring back at her. The fiend lingered in her closet doorway, with the full-figured body of a man, and a head so black that she could barely see if he had a face at all. As he shuffled out of the closet toward her, Donna noticed that "his fingers were like claws, long claws, and he had a neck." She froze at the edge of her bed. The man reached toward her and grabbed her arm. "Leave me alone! I'm not bothering you!" the fiend said, as Donna flew back into her body and opened her eyes in the physical world. She looked down at her arm. It was bruised where the brute had grabbed her. She knew instantly what he wanted—to have intercourse with her. This was her first contact with the "spirit of lust," as Donna referred to the invisible energy behind sexual violence.

"When he realized I wouldn't have sex with my flesh," Donna explained, "he came to me in spirit. He was having sex with me, and I felt like he was trying to put his seed in me."

At the time, Donna was so bothered by the experience of an incubus visiting her for intercourse that she confided in one of her girlfriend-neighbors. Her girlfriend suggested that she try confronting the demonic entity. "Next time you go to sleep, ask it to reveal itself!"

"So, one night, it came right up behind me, caressing me, stroking me. Felt like a man touching me. Lord have mercy! Who are you, I asked, and I turned around and looked. It had horns coming out of its head and eyes this big! It had bubbles, boils all over its face. I turned and said, 'I rebuke you in the name of Jesus. Get off of me, don't touch me!' Oh, yeah. And it did. It moved; it was losing its power over me. It kept slipping away, knowing it was losing power. The closer I got to God, the more it lost its power."

Each evening, Donna prayed to God to give her the power to defeat the spirit of lust in this world and in its parallel dimension. In fact, she fell into a nightly ritual of praying and reading the Bible, surmising that if the incubus saw her reading the scripture and praying for her family—"Lord, I want you to cover my children!"—he would be so upset that she had reclaimed her body that he would attack her in the spirit world once she went to sleep. And she was right. Once, after falling asleep, Donna awoke in the other world, sat on her bed, and decided to start looking for the beast herself. She stood up and walked out of her bedroom into the living room, which was empty. Then she turned to her bathroom and opened the door.

"I know you're here. Where are you?" Donna asked as she placed her celestial body in the bathtub to wait for him. Suddenly, the incubus attacked her from behind, clawing at her arms.

Donna stuck out her hands and felt a surge of power flow through her palms, releasing pulses of light in its direction. Each time she hit the fiend with light, it emitted an unearthly howl before eventually scampering off into the night. Donna was surprised by her power. The fire that had almost killed her as a little girl was becoming the basis of her protection.

With each successive journey into the spirit realm, Donna's confidence in her ability to defeat the spirit of lust in her life surged. She reasoned that the incubus was the thing behind the treatment of women as sexual property in society. If she could defeat supernatural sexism, she would stand a much better chance of maintaining her freedom from the earthly kind. And she maintained her spiritual routine of reading the scriptures and praying, often several times a day, to remain close to God.

One afternoon, after revisiting a favorite biblical passage, Donna decided to take a nap. As soon as she closed her eyes, she found herself in the spirit world, in the hallway of her apartment, facing the bathroom with her back toward the bedroom door. As she stood there, she felt an arm slither around her throat and yank her violently back into a headlock. Donna panicked as she struggled to breathe.

"Je . . . sus," she tried to utter, hoping his name would protect her as it had before. "Je . . . sus."

Donna couldn't quite get the word out of her mouth. The brute had targeted her throat for a reason. Donna tried to calm herself and think properly. Maybe she was going about this the wrong way. It only appeared that she possessed a physical body in the spirit realm. Why was she trying to breathe or even speak, anyway? Couldn't she just think her actions into being, as she had learned as a little girl in the house fire? She formed the word "Jesus" in her mind and, sure enough, the incubus howled and jerked his hand back from Donna's throat. And there, written on the inside of his palm, was the word "JESUS," in fire and flames. Donna was astonished. So, she thought to herself, in the spirit world one does not act in the flesh but in the mind. The incident taught Donna the protective power of telepathy. "Telepathy is good thing," she chuckled. "It has its advantages."

INCUBUS, THE FINAL BATTLE

As a novice in the spiritual world, Donna had received her first taste of supernatural warfare. Apparently the fantasies of men were not limited to the realm of flesh and bone. Misogynists and rapists haunted the borders of the immaterial, too. And because Donna now had one foot planted in the physical world and one slightly over the border to an unseen world, it took her several months to find her balance.

"I was being attacked every night by the spirit of lust, and this demon kept attacking me." Then, one evening, after she entered the spirit realm, she acquired more spiritual power, which appeared to be derived from the element of fire.

"God of Abraham, Isaac, and Jacob, give me the power to defeat this demon," Donna prayed internally as she woke up in the incorporeal realm. "In the spirit world all of a sudden, my body levitated above my bed. I feel myself rising up. Then I'm lying, like, horizontally, and I'm wise enough first to open my mouth. And I see this flame of fire coming through the ceiling going in my mouth, into my spirit. My mouth closes, then I levitate upward. Instead of laying down, I'm upright now, straight in the air. I hear the demon coming at me, and then all of a sudden, something tells me, 'Do this with your hand, do that' [she throws her fingers forward as if they are a wand], and then all of a sudden I see lightning coming off my fingers, and I'm hitting and I'm wounding it [the demon], and I'm saying, 'I'm not afraid of you. I fear my God more than I fear you!' I hear it. I don't see it, but I can tell I'm wounding it." In her moment of incandescence, Donna realized that God had empowered her spirit with the capacity to incinerate the demon. Finally the fiend exploded into nothingness and "the spirit of lust has never visited me since," Donna smiled at me, explaining that from that moment, she no longer felt desire for a man.

Although Donna had been mistreated and abused on the horizontal planes of this world for most of her life as a result of her status as a poor Black woman, in the spiritual world she now stood upright, vertical, and proud, her tongue filled with the fire of the Holy Ghost, her hands charged with a life force potent enough to repel any woman-hating visitor back to the abyss from which he came.

6

SEEDS OF EVIL

Donna overcame her fear of mammograms shortly after defeating the spirit of lust. It had been close to twenty-five years since the doctor who diagnosed her first cancer said that the disease might come back in a few decades, but Donna was confident of her good health, given that she was knee-deep in the Word of God. And she was right. Her first mammogram result was negative, and Donna sang the praises of the Lord all the way home. The following year, the same result, and the year after that, negative. So on the morning of her fourth mammogram, Donna woke up in a good mood, singing the Lord's praises, "Do to me as your will God. I am yours!"

Donna smiled and put on her good clothes. She wanted to make sure she made it to the hospital on time for her appointment, so she left the apartment early and jumped on the MBTA bus with a Bible in one hand and her compact disc player in the other, the inspiring sounds of Yolanda Adams flowing into her ears: "For whatever comes, I'm gone' be ready / Strength to pass any test / I feel like I'm so blessed / With you in control, I can't go wrong."[1]

Donna stepped down from the city bus in front of the hospital and made her way to the oncology department waiting room. "Why is everyone so sad today?" she asked with a smile, as she greeted other women waiting to be seen. "I was a ball of sunshine and I wanted to inspire people," she remembered. "When I went into the changing room, a lady came in crying. I said, 'Honey, you're are going to be alright. If He brought you to it, He is going to bring you through it. And I wiped away the tears from her face." Donna got changed and went into the mammogram screening room for her x-rays. The process went smoothly, and the nurse asked her to return to the waiting room. She was so happy, she "went out into the waiting room and started cracking jokes" with the other women waiting for their test results. It felt so good to see their smiling faces and to be a part of the reason their moods improved as they laughed.

One by one, each woman was called in to see the doctor and then allowed to leave, until Donna was the only one left in the waiting room. That's when it hit her that something was amiss.

A nurse walked in. "Ms. Donna Haskins, the doctor will see you now. She would like to take another x-ray."

Donna stood up with a lump of nerves in her throat and walked into the mammogram screening room, where she immediately noticed an x-ray of her breast with a dark spot in the middle. Donna sighed deeply without panicking. "I'm not going to worry about something that I don't know. I don't need to worry. I'm trusting in God," she repeated to herself over and over. After her second x-ray, Donna's doctor confirmed that there was indeed a strange mass in her breast, and she would need to come back in a week for a biopsy.

"We will make a small incision in your breast and take a sample of the mass to make sure it is benign," explained the doctor.

"I'm not going to worry about something that I don't know," Donna told herself, as she left the oncologist's office and made her way to the bus stop to return home.

A week later her oncologist took three tissue samples from Donna's breast, stitched her back up, and asked her to wait another week for the pathology report. The following week Donna received a call from her primary care doctor. The tests came back positive. Donna had breast cancer. "If there was a type of breast cancer I would want you to have, this would not be the one," her doctor admitted over the phone, as Donna faded in and out of shock. Her physician's words seemed to slow down and muddle together. Just as she had begun to experience her body as a host of divine power, the evils of her past had returned.

"Donna, I am going to give you the best," her doctor assured her over the telephone. "We are going to remove that lump and do our best for you. We need to schedule you for surgery in the next two weeks. Please make an appointment with Dr. Rubin in oncology." Donna hung up the phone and cried.

Two days later she received another phone call from her primary care doctor. "Is everything okay? I'm worried. How are you feeling, Donna?" her physician asked.

"I'm just fine," Donna responded, feeling as though she was the one calming her doctor's nerves rather than the other way around.

Two days later her primary called again. "Donna, how are you feeling?"

"My doctor was looking at the science, and it worried her. I had the perspective of spirit, so she didn't panic me with her fear. It didn't affect me," Donna explained. "I believed that my cancer was the result of the spirit of lust putting his seeds in me, when he tried to rape me in the spirit world," she added, echoing the trauma of her first cancer diagnosis shortly after she had been raped by Scooter.

Donna's spiritual perspective, however, allowed her to keep a sense of humor when she showed up to have her lump removed. "I don't need these breasts anymore!" she told the operating room attendees, saying she was celibate. "You can take them. Nobody ain't going to be sucking on these things no more anyway. I don't use 'em."

Everyone laughed. "No, no, Ms. Haskins. We don't do that anymore. You get to keep your breast," one of the surgeons assured her.

"Oh, thank you, Jesus!" sighed Donna, who in all seriousness had come to accept the possibility that she might require a full mastectomy. "Let me sit down then [on the operating table]."

CHEMO

Donna's surgeons successfully removed the lump—the size of the tip of a ballpoint pen—in her breast, and it was so small, her oncologist recommended four chemo treatments rather than the usual eight required for Donna's type of breast cancer. Two weeks later she arrived at the hospital for her chemo, accompanied by her daughters Alexis and Joy. Joy was home from college for the summer and promised her mother she would remain by her side for all the treatments.

When Donna sat down to receive her first chemo, she saw four tubes of thick red liquid "that looked like blood" attached to an intravenous needle. "I weighed about 230 pounds at the time, so they explained that to match my weight, I had to have four tubes of chemo pumped into my arm." As the toxic liquid dripped into her veins, she suddenly began to feel itchy all over, and her skin burned as it turned a reddish color.

"Alexis, I think I'm allergic to chemo," Donna looked over at her daughter, as her breath shortened.

Alexis yelled for the nurse. "I think my mother is allergic to the chemo!"

The nurses came rushing into the room and immediately began pumping Donna with an antihistamine and steroids as she became overwhelmed with emotion. "How can I be allergic to chemo!" she cried. "Oh my God, what are we going to do? How am I going to treat this cancer if I can't take chemo?"

"It's no problem, Ms. Haskins," the nurses assured Donna. "For your next treatment, we will just have to premedicate you."

Donna felt like she was eighty-five years old by the time she made it home that day. Walking up the stairs wore her out, and when she entered her apartment, she went straight to her bedroom, shut the door, tossed her body onto the mattress, and began talking to God.

"What is Nana saying?" Alexis' daughter asked her mother, as Donna's immediate family members sat in the living room.

"I think she is speaking to God," answered Alexis, trying to catch a phrase or two. The effort was futile, since Donna's words had transitioned to divine speech as she lay on the bed, a flow of incomprehensible syllables even the speaker could not fully understand.

One moment Donna had been praising God for helping her make it through her first treatment. The next, "tongues started coming out of me." It was the first time she ever experienced her "tongues" of fire, and, ironically, the healing gift of divine speech came to her while she was deathly ill. But from that moment on, speaking the language of the spirit world on occasion "became so natural and just rolled out of me."

Before her second chemo treatment, Donna was premedicated in her own private hospital room, which had a television, refrigerator, and bed. She had to arrive very early in the morning, and by the time she finished her dose of steroids, antihistamine, and chemo, it was very late in the day. This time Donna's fatigue had worsened, and her body trembled from anxiety and mental distress. She was especially distraught by the color of her hands and feet, which had become darkened, rough, and gritty to the touch, and her fingers had turned a reddish black. And because of the constant diet of steroids, nausea pills, and anxiety medication, Donna was gaining tons of weight, even as she lost all her beautiful, thick, black and silvering hair. Moreover, when Donna wasn't receiving chemo, she spent all day curled up on her bed behind closed doors, her cat, Smokey, near her pillow, the warmth of her fur caressing Donna's bald head.

"My cat, Smokey, never wanted me to touch her," noted Donna. "But for some reason during my chemo treatments, she placed her body right on the back of my head. Whenever she did it, I always felt like it was Jesus touching me on the back of my head, telling me he loved me."

Donna slept so much between chemo treatments that one time she woke to find her daughter Joy holding a mirror up to her mouth, "to see if she was still breathing."

"What are you doing?" asked Donna, startled.

"Mommy, you have been sleeping all day. I just wanted to make sure you were still alive," said Joy, exasperated.

"Yes, Joy, I'm still alive," Donna smiled at her younger girl, thinking that, from now on, she would let out a cough once in a while, so she didn't have to wake up to a mirror in her face.

On the morning of her fourth bout with chemo, Donna could no longer be strong for her daughters. Just the thought of allowing nurses to pump four more tubes of red toxins into her body, the steroids, the pills, and the fatigue made her so angry at the world around her, even at the people she cared for most.

"I just want to be by myself!" Donna lashed out at Joy as they reached the hospital's lobby elevators. "Just leave me alone. Just go away. Just go!"

Donna stepped onto the elevator and left her daughter standing in the hallway. When Donna reached the floor of the oncology department, though, Joy was there waiting to receive her.

"Mommy, you're not going to get rid of me. I told you I was gonna be with you the whole way through your treatment, and I ain't stopping now," she said.

"Joy, I'm sorry. I'm just so tired," Donna teared up.

"I understand, Mommy," Joy held her mother. "This is your last treatment. You did it!"

"No, we did it," whispered Donna.

Joy looked into her mother's eyes. "Let's go show them what Haskinses got. Let's go do it!" With Joy by her side, Donna allowed the chemo to enter her body that day and walked out of the hospital with her head held high, even knowing that in a couple of weeks she would have to return to undergo the next phase of her plan: radiation.

RADIATION

Each time she visited Faulkner Hospital, Donna felt as though she was the only Black woman with large breasts receiving radiation among all the women gathered there. "We were like a family of women," she Donna. "We would sit and compare our stories and diagnoses and sometimes laugh together. For example, I met a British woman who came to be with her daughter who was having radiation treatments. Everyone knew everyone. We would pray for each other, and especially when a regular woman who had cancer no longer showed up for her appointments. There was one lady that was having radiation for brain cancer that I came to know. And everyone would comfort me because they knew that because of my skin pigmentation and large breasts, I would burn over a larger area of skin and faster than others."

The radiation room was bone-chillingly cold to offset the heat of the machine. During treatments, Donna was required to lay on a flat, narrow bed under the radiation apparatus with fishnet material over her breast, and she was told to avert her eyes away from the intense laser as it burned the same spot on her breast five days a week, six and a half weeks in a row.

During the fourth week of treatment, Donna wiped under her breast during a morning shower and noticed globs of thin brown material coming off into her hand. When she realized that it was her skin, she jumped out of the shower screaming, "What? What?" Lifting up her breast to the mirror, she was horrified. Her breast without skin was raw and painful. Layers of skin were drooping off and cracking into her hand.

At the hospital the next day, Donna's radiologist assured her that her raw breast was normal, and that dead skin would need to peel off during treatments. He gave her a kit of bandages, gauze, sanitizing spray, tubes of burn ointment, and tweezers so that she could peel off the dead skin on her own time and treat the burns. Donna's breast burned all the way from her chest cavity to the side of her body, and the pain was so unbearable that she couldn't wear a wired bra.

"I didn't let my kids know that I was being burned like that. I sat up when my kids came over and put up a front. I wanted something so bad to take away the pain. They gave me Percocet, and two hours later the pain would be back. So I turned to the Lord," Donna began sobbing audibly as we spoke. "'I'm not asking you to take it away, Lord. Just give me the strength to bear it," she begged, identifying with Jesus's suffering on the cross. "Please don't take it away, give me the strength to bear it. Jesus, I need to sleep," she cried. "And I fell asleep. I went into a deep sleep, and the next day I was able to endure it."

The day of Donna's final radiation was the worst. "This machine is burning me. I am literally being burnt, and I sat on the edge of the bed and said, 'God, I don't want to go. I'm going to call on you. Please give me the strength, because I can't do it by myself.' I sat on the edge of the bed crying and feeling the pain in my breast. I said, 'Okay, Donna, let's get it together. You gotta get the radiation done.' I lifted my head up and smiled, and I said, 'Satan, you lose, you lose, you lose!' So I got on that bus and left my house at ten and got there an hour late. And they were so nice to me when I got there late (Donna starts crying as she remembers). And the lady who had an eleven o'clock appointment told me to go right ahead. And when I got into the radiation room, they had never seen me so broken before, and I think it really touched them, that I had been trying to be strong the whole time, and now I was broken. They held my hand the whole time. They said: 'We know we are hurting you, but you gotta do what you gotta do.' And they were all crying. They said, 'Donna, this is your last one.' And that was it!" She had successfully made it through her radiation treatments.

A few days later when Donna went to visit her primary care doctor, the young woman took one look at her breast and cried. "Donna, this a second-degree burn! You should have been hospitalized. What were they doing?" she said with tears in her eyes, looking away. Donna knew her doctor was right. Her oldest daughter knew it, too, and cussed out a few nurses for not treating her mother's pain properly—a far too common occurrence with Black patients receiving medical care at predominately white hospitals.[2] Donna wasn't sure how she endured so much pain.

"I wanted to be so strong for my kids. I didn't want them to see me weak. And I wanted them to see God's power in me. And that I am not alone, and I could do anything if He's with me."

"Where do we go from here?" Donna asked her primary care physician.

"Well, you have to go through a series of tests to make sure all the cancer is gone. And you have to come back every year after that to make sure it remains in remission," Donna's doctor explained.

"By the grace of God, everything was fine with my tests," said Donna. "And every year I went back for tests I was still in remission." But then, she sighed, "The third year, there was another spot on my x-rays in the same breast."

Donna had been poring over the Word of God and praying in her apartment the day before her x-ray, when she felt the presence of the Holy Spirit and a voice suggest that she fast from food for a week. After her yearly mammogram, however, her doctor requested an MRI and biopsy the following day and instructed her to take medication with food prior to the operation. Initially she debated whether to disobey her doctor's orders, but then she thought better of it and swallowed her medicine with food. An hour later Donna found herself staring into a toilet bowl, vomiting everything up.

"I guess the Holy Spirit was going to make sure I fasted!" she chuckled.

The next day Donna went to the hospital for the MRI and the biopsy on an empty stomach, unsure if she had actually ingested the medication, but she placed her trust in God.

During the MRI, Donna decided to try something new based on her recent flights into the spirit realm. If it worked at night when she closed her eyes, why couldn't it work during the day, when she was fully awake inside an MRI machine? Maybe she could leave her body in the machine, while her spirit floated above in an unseen part of the hospital room until the MRI was complete.

"Don't touch me. Whatever you do, when I am in the MRI machine, do not touch me!" Donna was adamant as she prepared to enter the apparatus.

"Okay, Donna, no problem, I won't touch you," the nurse helping her said, confusedly.

Donna entered the machine, closed her eyes, and asked the Holy Spirit to take her into the spirit realm. "Wow, this is so cool," she thought to herself, as she floated above the MRI machine, looking down. "Cool, I can leave my body," she snapped her fingers in delight.

"I was like, 'Hey, I can do this!'" beamed Donna. "I was able to see the angels in the room and everything. I was so excited. I could also hear the nurse asking me if I was okay. I was watching them, and I was just fine. Then I guess they got worried, because I wasn't responding when they asked me if I was okay. I guess they started to think something was wrong with me and the lady touched me. As soon as she did that, I flew right into my body, and I screamed at her, 'Didn't I tell you don't touch me! Didn't I tell you don't touch me!' I felt so bad for the lady afterward for yelling at her, I had to apologize. I went right up to her later and said, 'I'm sorry for yelling at you.' She looked at me like I was crazy, but I couldn't really explain to her why I asked her not to touch me. I told her, 'Honey, it's going to go right over your head,'" laughed Donna.

After her MRI, Donna's biopsy procedure went smoothly, and Donna's doctor asked her to wait almost a week to learn if her cancer had returned. Donna went home and remained true to her fast, not eating for at least another six days to draw nearer to the Holy Spirit. Then, on Monday morning, the phone rang. It was Donna's primary care physician.

"Donna, the results from your biopsy have come in," her doctor began. "The tumor was benign." Donna's heart soared. She was cancer free.

Donna thanked her doctor and hung up the phone. As she looked around her living room, she repeated, "God is good. God is good." There was no way, she thought, God would have brought her this far, only to abandon her now.

7

CHRYSALIS

There is a basin in the mind where words float around on thought and thought on sound and sight. Then there is a depth of thought untouched by words, and deeper still a gulf of form-less feelings untouched by thought. Nanny entered this infinity of conscious pain again on her old knees.

—Zora Neale Hurston, *Their Eyes Were Watching God*

The quality of Donna's interior life could no longer be determined by her environment. Through its recurring incarnation in her mind, the Holy Spirit adorned Donna with a new consciousness, beyond the confines of societal perceptions of and violence against her body. She had become more interested in the "things behind the things," astounded by her fantastic ability to speak in tongues, to perform telepathy, and to channel fire to explode dangerous configurations of power haunting her American neighborhood. As a little girl, Donna had always been awestruck by the destructive nature of fire, but she was slowly learning how to harness its energy to actualize her true identity as a conduit of light.

To further her spiritual growth, Donna decided to visit Joy's grandmother, Mother Irie, in her Roxbury home for guidance. Mother Irie was a holy woman from Jamaica, whom Donna admired for her love of Jesus. When Donna was dating DeAngelo years earlier, Mother Irie had called her aside, peered into her eyes, and asked in her beautiful Jamaican patois, "Girl, do ya love Jesus?" Mother Irie also prophesied that Donna would overcome her battle with cancer, so when she enjoined her to participate in a candle lightening ceremony to worship the Holy Spirit, Donna obliged.

When Donna arrived, the table in Mother Irie's apartment basement had been "made up like an offering to the Holy Spirit," with colorful fruit well-arranged and unlit candles on top of tin cans placed around the perimeter for each worship participant. The invocation for the Holy Spirit to descend into the room went out through Mother Irie's prayer as the room grew silent. Then, one by one, each person lit the candle before her as someone in the room offered a warning.

"Be careful what you pray for."

Donna slowly leaned over the fire, its light dancing in the dimness of the room. Then she spoke in her mind. "I want to see Jesus," she prayed.

Donna went home and barely remembered her prayer. Three months later, however, she was sitting on the edge of her bed, thinking about all she had overcome, her multiple suicide attempts, segregated schools, illiteracy, unemployment, poor housing, the death of her nephews, breast cancer, asthma, being sexually assaulted, the men who cheated on her, and her promise of abstinence to the Lord. "No man should have dominion over me," she said. "I should never have given them dominion over me. I should not have handed it to them as if I was giving them my birth certificate. So now, I'm getting my birth certificate back. I'm getting everything back—my mind, my heart, my soul," she prayed.

This was Donna's "covenant" with the Lord, as she looked down at the floor. Indeed, she was still purging herself of the past, and sometimes it felt good to cry out to God.

"Lord, I'm hurting," she said out loud. "I'm hurting. I'm not going to break my promise. Heal my broken heart." Then, slowly, Donna laid back and drifted off the sleep. The next time she woke up, she found herself in the spirit world, where she would meet Jesus for the first time.

SECOND WORK OF GRACE: MEETING JESUS

Donna paused for an eternity before relaying this part of her story. Tears began to flow from her eyes, and it became clear that what she was about to describe to me was the most sacred moment of her life.

"Every time I speak of this story, I can't say it without feeling emotional, because every time, oh Lord. Jesus," Donna's voice fluttered. "Every time. Oh Lord, every time. Thank you, angels. Thank you for being with me now. Oh Lord, Jesus. You've got to understand what I was going through hurt me so bad. Every time I go there, it just hurts. But God, He was there. He came there. The Lord showed up. Oh Lord, He showed up. I got lifted out of my bed. I got put to the floor. And I saw my floor, my hands were shaking."

Donna is suddenly moved to speak in tongues as I watch her trembling body. "Excuse me, Onaje. Jesus. He's touching me right now. Yes Jesus, take it away. Take it. Oh Lord, Jesus, take it away, God. Take it away," she cried, as if each time Jesus touched her, he sent a shock wave of electric love through her being, removing sorrow from her soul.

Donna seemed to enter into an unseen reality as she spoke. "Oh Jesus, oh Lord. Oh Jesus. Oh Lord, help me, Jesus. Yes Lord, I hear you. I hear you Father. Yes Father. Yes, God. Oh, Lord."

Then Donna became calm again and slowly began to explain to me what happened to her that evening she met Jesus in the spirit world.

"My floor turned to water. I saw his face in the water. And then I said, 'Jesus, is that you?' And then the face disappeared. The next thing I knew, it was like the moon was reflecting on the water. It made me think about when Jesus walked on water, and Peter came out of the boat. The water looked like that.[1] And then, all of a sudden, the water disappeared, and I see the floor again. And I hear the Lord speak to me. I was in a bowing position. I mean, I was laying forward like I was bowing to a king, and I realized that I couldn't move, and that made me get nervous and scared because sometimes the enemy will come at you when you're paralyzed, when you can't move. So, when I couldn't move, I thought that it was the enemy manipulating me. And then all of a sudden, I was able to move, and I heard the voice, and I heard a voice say to me, 'My child, please stand up.' And I didn't stand up right away. I saw the hem of his garment. I saw the hem of the garment. It was white. And He had to say it to me again. 'My child, please stand up.' He literally had to say it three times. I was so afraid to stand up because of all the stuff that I had done in my life that was bad that I've told you about. I thought it was Judgment Day for me [starts crying]. I thought it was Judgment Day, but I said, 'You know what? I did it. And if this is Judgment Day, then it is God's will. It's God's will. There's nothing I can do. It's God's will.' And then I stood up."

"And when I stood up, all of a sudden, every sin I did came out my mouth. And I could see the sins that I did. And it was coming out of my mouth, and I could see it at the same time. And then Jesus took his hand up in front of my mouth and just stopped, and I stopped."

Donna then turned to me directly, as if she had come back from an unseen world. "Onaje, just as I speak to you right now, there are six angels with me. They're getting the enemy away from me, because they're trying to come at me. I can see them. They're with me right now. They [the enemy] don't want me to tell the story."

Then Donna continued, "Then Jesus put his hand up, and I just stopped. He was speaking to me mind-to-mind. And he was telling me, 'My daughter, I have been with you today, and I will be with you until the end of time.' He was telling me that 'I will not leave you or forsake you, my daughter.' He kept calling me his daughter," revealed Donna, reminiscent of the way the glowing man in the house fire cared for her when she was five years old. "He told me he loved me. Oh my God, he told me he loved me. He was telling me he loved me, and he had forgiven all my sins. He was standing there. He was just standing there. He wasn't talking. He wouldn't move his mouth. His eyes were so beautiful. They were sparkling like light and diamonds. He wasn't even moving his mouth. Oh my God. I wanted to stay with Him."

"He then began pouring love into me. After he had spoken to me, he reached his arms out to me. He brought me into His bosoms, and I felt all this love come inside me, a love that I can't even express. It's not a love of this world. It's not the love of my mother, my father, my sister, my brothers, my kids, and my grandkids. It's an indescribable love that you can't make into sense. It was like a never-ending love that kept going on and on. The love was getting greater and greater and stronger and stronger."

"And the next thing I did, I fell to the floor, and before I fell to the floor, He was standing in front of me, and there was an angel behind me because I could see its white fingers. I was literally in the Lord's arms, and I was crying on his shoulders like a baby. I was pulling all of the hurt that was in me out of me into Him, and He was taking it all. And I was laying on his shoulder, and as I had my head turned to the left, I could see the hands (of the angel), white fingers on my left shoulder, and it was just holding me, and I was just wrapped in all this love. All this love I was wrapped in. The angel wasn't saying nothing. The Lord wasn't saying nothing. And the next thing I know, I fell to the floor. I just fell back, and I hit the floor. As I looked up, I could see Jesus standing over me, and I could see this power, lightning, coming out of the tips of Jesus's fingers, coming out of the palms of His hands, and it was just hitting me, and I saw him hit me four times [with lightning], and I was laying there like I was having a seizure. It was like I was having an epileptic seizure, and all I was doing was just looking up at Him, and as He was hitting me [with the lightning], He was smiling. He was smiling the whole time he was hitting me, and I was receiving. I didn't say anything. I didn't speak. I couldn't speak. My mouth was silent. When he moved his hands, he silenced me, and I couldn't say nothing."

Then, suddenly, it was over.

Donna returned from the Spirit realm to her physical body and sat up on the edge of her bed. "Jesus was here. He was here!"

Donna jumped off her bed and touched the floor where she had bowed to Jesus in a pool of water. "The floor felt warm, and I said he was here!"

Off and on for the next several days, she lay on that spot, only getting up to eat and go to the bathroom. If being given a new mind by the Holy Spirit months earlier had been her first blessing, Donna had now been baptized in a pool of water and lightning by Jesus with her "second blessing," or what some Holiness Christian traditions refer to, interchangeably, as being gifted with "Perfect Love, Heart Purity, Entire Sanctification, Full Salvation, or Christian Perfection." "In the experience of entire sanctification," one writer explains,

> there is a second inward change. . . . Whereas, the first is the birth of the Spirit . . . the second is baptism with the Spirit, in which he receives the purifying of his heart . . . the first removes the shoots of sin: the second the roots of sin; the first deals with sin as a practice in the outward life: the second deals with sin as a principle in the heart . . . the first gives us life, the second gives us "life more abundant"; the first gives us love: the second gives us "perfect love that casteth out fear"; the first gives us "peace with God," the second gives us "the peace of God"; . . . the first gives

us a new heart: the second gives us a pure heart; the first gives us a right to heaven; the second gives us the fitness for heaven.[2]

After this "second work of grace," through Jesus, the spirit world just "opened up to me," noticed an astonished and grateful Donna. She had arrived at a remarkable stage of spiritual maturity, which seemed to crack open the gates of the spirit realm perpetually.

"One minute I was here, and the next minute, the spirit world was opened up to me. I could be sitting here, and I'd just fall asleep, and when I think I'm waking up, I'm actually waking up into the spirit world. That's how fast it happens. It's like in the blink of an eye."

After her encounter with Jesus it was "weird to be in the spirit world all the time," Donna admitted. "I always wondered when I traveled there, 'what are they going to show me now?' I was always excited, because I knew the Holy Spirit was going to teach me something. Every time I went there, it was an adventure."

In the beginning, Donna's family, especially her daughters, didn't understand why she spent almost all her time in her bedroom exploring this other dimension. "Why are you always in the spirit world?" they asked her, over and over.

"I would have to explain to them all the time," Donna said, "that the world of spirit is always open to me. Who am I to shut it out? It's always there."

CHILD OF LIGHT

A few months after her encounter with Jesus, the Holy Spirit also visited Donna to reveal her true identity.

"The Holy Spirit came to me one night and woke me up at like 3:00 a.m. and revealed my true name. 'My child, you'll be called Child of Light now,' the Holy Spirit revealed. Now, whenever the angels talk to me, they call me My Child or Child of Light. Demons, on the other hand, cannot resist calling me Donna, because Donna is a name that was given to me on earth by my mother and not by the Holy Spirit. Remember that something similar happened to Abraham in the Bible?[3] The Holy Spirit changed my name into Child of Light. Why? Because I am made out of light. Some people who have the gift to see into the spirit world recognize that I am made of light. My sister's husband, who has the gift of sight, confirmed it. He said: 'Sis, you know what you look like in the spirit? You're made out of light.' Others have said, 'You have this light coming out of your heart, and it comes out of you, and the enemy attempts to blow out your light, but they cannot. You have long white hair in the spirit.' The best way I can describe who I look like in the spirit world, Onaje, is Halle Berry in the movie *X-Men*, where she plays Storm. That is what my hair looks like in the spirit world. And my body floats in the spirit world."

This made perfect sense to me, maybe not in a neat Christian universe, but in a supernatural realm that was tantalizingly complex and imbued with Afro-Caribbean elements. Donna's stages of spiritual growth were obviously drawn from the religious grammar of Christian Holiness traditions (even though she was Baptist and born Catholic) as she moved from regeneration in the Holy Spirit toward perfection in Christ. But at the same time, through Mother Irie and her own Afro-Jamaican roots, Donna's lived religion included floating in and out of her body, and she embraced the element of fire as a natural manifestations of God's presence, as if it, too, could mediate the divine. This explained why fire seemed to be always paired with Donna's experiences of the supernatural, right down to the electric color of her hair. Although Jesus and the Holy Spirit might be in control of Donna's universe, their presence in her body was manifest through flames. Donna believed that she possessed a natural kinship with fire as if they were lit from the same vibrational source, or, as she told me once, "I'm a walking candle." And now Jesus and the Holy Spirit had helped her to reclaim the purity of her original essence from the darkness of Boston's neighborhoods. After all, hadn't Jesus proclaimed: "I am the light of the world. Whoever follows me will never walk in darkness, but will have the light of life."[4]

Donna's beautiful mind and spiritual maturity also helped me to understand how someone who lived on a fixed income in subsidized housing and negotiated racism and sexism daily in Roxbury could carry herself with the dignity of a royal. Over the four years I had come to know her as she negotiated poverty, I witnessed Donna labor in the spirit realm on behalf of dozens of people without ever expecting anything monetary in return. And when pay was offered on occasion, she just smiled, and explained, "No thank you, I don't accept money from people for helping them. What was given to me is a gift. How can I charge? God takes care of me." Donna believed that the wealth of her interior life was worth far more than anything the world had to offer.

She described her majesty this way: "One night, I looked up, and I saw men with long beards on my ceiling, and the phrase, 'elders of the church came to me,' as they looked down on me. I heard them talking when I woke up in the spirit realm, and I was afraid to move because they were talking, and I wanted to honor them by not interrupting what they were doing. I didn't think they knew I was awake as I lay still, but actually, they knew I heard them praising me. They were praising me as if I was a queen! I heard them repeat to me, 'The glory of the Lord is on your shoulders. The glory of the Lord is on your shoulders.'"

III

CHILD OF LIGHT

8

BETWEEN WORLDS

The glory of the Lord imbued Donna with a luminescence so that she had become a walking candle for
those with eyes to see her halo. And sure enough,
supernatural beings from all over the cosmos began visiting her
Roxbury apartment in multitudes, often unannounced, turning
her one-bedroom flat into a bridge between worlds.

Initially, after her encounter with Jesus in a pool of water on
the floor of her bedroom, Donna felt as though she had entered
the border of an unusual territory with strange geography and
inhabitants. She wondered, how vast was this spiritual world?
And who lived there? How could she identify the differences
between an entity that was good and one that was evil? And why

was she invited? These questions were daunting for such a novice, but Donna did take solace in the knowledge that after his baptism, Jesus also entered unfamiliar territory.[1]

"Jesus was in the wilderness when he got baptized by John the Baptist. He knew he had to go and defeat Satan. He knew he had to go. He went in the woods. So, what makes you think that we ain't supposed to be in the wilderness? How are we gonna learn? He [God] can't hold our hand all the time. He can't do it for us all the time. We have to do for ourselves."

EARTHBOUND SPIRITS

One of Donna's first visitors from the spirit world was a young woman from the bottom of Boston's social ladder, who had recently been killed by her pimp. One evening, as Donna awoke in the spirit realm, she noticed the sex worker sitting on the edge of her bed wearing a seductive blue teddy.

"Who are you?" Donna asked, quite surprised to see the half-dressed young lady staring back at her.

"I used to be a prostitute," she said nervously. "My pimp murdered me. I don't know where to go. Is it okay if I stay here?"

"I can't help you," Donna said kindly, speaking to the dead for the first time. "I don't know how, but you can come back and visit me if you want," she encouraged. Sure enough, for the following three evenings, each time Donna awoke in the spirit realm, she found the same young woman sitting at the edge of her bed, wearing her sexy blue teddy.

Spirits of other deceased people turned up at Donna's apartment as well. One evening an older man scared her almost half to death when he ran into her bedroom and hid behind the dresser. "Get out of here!" she hollered as she sat up in the spirit realm, causing him to bolt from his hiding spot and scamper through her door.

The following day Donna visited a neighbor in an adjacent apartment whom she had recently befriended, and, astonishingly, she recognized a man in one of the photographs the woman had on her mantle.

"Donna, I know I haven't told you, but my husband was hit by a car three years ago and died," the neighbor revealed, picking up the photograph of her husband standing with several other people.

"Wait a minute, don't point him out," Donna pleaded, staring at the photo. "Is that your husband right there?" she asked, as the woman's eyes grew wide and a perplexed expression flashed across her face.

"How did you know?"

Donna smiled, realizing now that spirits of the dead were being drawn to her aura. "When you open up to that world, you start attracting all these beings to you, Onaje."

The spirits of deceased people living in the wilderness of Roxbury were so drawn to Donna that they even followed her when she wasn't at home. Once, at Roxbury Foods Grocery Store, she suddenly heard the shouting of loud voices as she perused the meat department with her daughter, Alexis. On her left, Donna saw two little boys following their mother around the store, but neither of the boys nor the mother was speaking, so it couldn't have been them.

"Who are the people shouting in the grocery store?" Donna turned to ask her daughter. "Why are they so loud?"

"Mommy, I don't hear anything. No one is being loud," Alexis responded, looking at her mother strangely.

Then, suddenly, Donna heard the voices again. "You can hear me? You can hear me!" one of them yelled, the voice coming from an invisible presence.

"Oh no, not in the grocery store!" Donna screamed, snatching her daughter's hand and running for the exits. As they made it outside, Donna cupped her hands over her ears and screamed, "Stop it! Shut up, Shut up! I don't want to hear it!"

The women reached their car. Alexis jumped into the driver's seat while Donna entered the opposite side. "I don't know who you are, and I can't help you. Go away," she ordered, as Alexis placed the key in the ignition and sped down Washington Avenue.

Later that evening, after Donna had dinner, she retired to her bedroom for the night, where she drifted off to sleep but then woke a few minutes later in the spirit world.

"I'm in the realm," she explained, "and I go into my living room, and I see all these people standing in the living room. I see a father, mother, and son watching my TV. But when I went to sleep, my TV was off. So I'm gathering whoever it was in the grocery store came home with me that night and sat down to watch some TV."

Apparently, ghosts of nuclear families weren't the only ones interested in watching their favorite programs on Donna's television. On another occasion she slipped off her flesh only to find several spirits hanging out on her living room couch watching television in the middle of the night. Donna simply shook her head, turned around, and slid back into her sleeping body. When she awoke in the real world, she jumped out of her bed and ran into the living room, only to find her lights off and the television untouched.

"I don't know who you are!" she grumbled. "But I can't help you!"

Donna stormed back into her bedroom and fell asleep on her pillow. A few minutes later she found herself in the spirit world again, only to hear the television on and a few of Boston's disinherited spirits chatting on her couch.

"I go back to sleep, and there they are again," she observed. "One of the dudes was in a gang, and he was saying for me to help him. He had a tear drop in his eye, and he kept saying, '*Mamacita, mamacita*, hey mommy!' And someone in his group said to him, 'Didn't she tell you not to ask for help!'"

Donna had no clue how to help these ghosts on the margins of the spirit world, but she did muster the courage one evening to ask a particularly lost apparition why she continued to wander the earth after death.

"This young girl appeared in my house. She said that she was lost, looking for her parents," revealed Donna. "I said to her, 'What are you doing here?' She said to me that she was lost, and I realized that this young girl didn't know that she was dead. So I said to her, 'Why didn't you go to the light?' And she responded that someone told her not to go into the light."

As a result of her conversation with the lost spirit girl, Donna learned two new pieces of information about the spirit realm. The first was that it was inhabited, in part, by wandering ghosts of individuals who believed they were still alive. Donna would come to refer to these ethereal wanderers, many of whom came from the bottom of Boston's social ladder while they were living, as earthbound spirits—that is, "someone who has died but is not able to cross over to the other world." The second piece of wisdom—besides the fact that the spirit realm seemed to be intimately connected to the physical world of everyday life—was that there must be a class of evil spirits who sometimes manipulated earthbound spirits to remain on earth rather than move into the light. "Maybe some evil spirit got the little girl to trust her,"

thought Donna, as she contemplated who might have misdi-
rected the little girl from the light and how to empower her to
cross over now.

Meeting the lost little girl and others like her also raised
another question in Donna's mind as she became more familiar
with the spiritual world. How would she discern the difference
between an earthbound spirit who was simply lost and one that
was still being manipulated by a demon toward some other evil
end? Contemplating this question caused Donna to label another
class of beings in the other world, which she referred to as "unfamiliar spirits."

"Unfamiliar spirits are someone who has died but who is also
being manipulated by demons to cause havoc while remaining
on earth," explained Donna. In other words, unfamiliar spirits
were dead persons being forced to harm the living against their
will. They are not "demons per se," she clarified. "They are negative spirits of people who were once living and have since died
in the flesh. Unfamiliar spirits don't always make the living
uncomfortable right away because they are not necessarily
demonic, but they are unclean and unfamiliar. Often they carry
the spirit of fear, the spirit of anger, or the spirit of greed with
them. It is difficult to tell how Satan may use them to interfere
in your life. You never really know. So I call them unfamiliar
spirits because we have not yet given them a title until it emerges.
It takes time to make sense of them."

"One of the differences between unfamiliar spirits and
demons," Donna continued, "is that demons cannot mask their
intentions like unfamiliar spirits. Unfamiliar spirits have lived
in the flesh before and can often speak a human language even
after their flesh has died. Whatever language you spoke when
you were living, you will be able to speak when you die. If you
spoke Spanish, you're going to speak Spanish after you die. There

are times I have come across Latino spirits, and they were trying to communicate with me in Spanish, but I don't speak Spanish. So I couldn't communicate with them, but they'll try. Now,
a demon, an evil spirit that has never lived in the flesh, cannot
speak Spanish. But it'll benefit the demon if it gets an unfamiliar spirit who speaks Spanish," she winked.

As Donna walked around Boston's inner-city streets, she
began to encounter earthbound and unfamiliar spirits all the
time, many of whom lived tragic lives and were now experiencing turmoil in the spirit realm. Some had even lived in isolated
housing projects like Donna's Columbia Point and had been
murdered, forgotten, and were now haunting their former
neighborhoods.

"I remember there was a killing not far from me where I used
to live, off of Dudley Street. I walked through the area, and I
felt the person who got killed—his spirit there. I literally felt that
spirit. And I walked through the area, and there was no memorial, no shrine or nothing, but I said—someone died here. This
person is angry. This person wants revenge. Sure enough, about
a year later, someone died on that same spot, that same spot that
I felt the presence of that person. They—I said—they see someone mourning for them and crying over them, you know, taking
their death really hard. And they want their death revenged.
They torment that living spirit, that person in the flesh, and
get them to avenge their death."

One of the places Donna began to notice spirits whom Toni
Morrison famously referred to in *Beloved* as the "black and angry
dead" was on Roxbury street corners, near makeshift shrines for
young men and women who had died far before their time.[2] Near
the teddy bears, candles, and handwritten notes left for the
deceased, Donna was conscious of furious spirits whispering in
the ears of loved ones.

"I see spirits who have passed away and got killed in street violence, wanting to avenge their deaths. They will go to the weakest [living] person in that group and be on them so much that that person will avenge their death. I've been where I've came through the city and saw shrines and will see the dead person's spirit talking to one of their friends, standing there crying, wanting that person to avenge their death. And it will be an ongoing cycle."

This "spirit of death" even sustained the criminal justice system. "I went to the Roxbury courthouse one time, and I saw the spirit of death. I kept seeing him follow three boys, individual boys, and I said death is calling them, and I had to walk out of the courthouse and start praying for those three boys' souls that I saw. These murdered spirits sometimes go to the weakest link, the one who's grieving the most for them, the one who wants to avenge them." Watching young Black and Latinx children being manipulated by unfamiliar spirits was, in part, how Donna came to understand how certain banished realities haunt social institutions and the people attempting to survive within them.

In her foreword to Avery Gordon's *Ghostly Matters*, Janice Radway describes the role of the apparently dead and forgotten among the living this way: "Gordon believes sociology must seek also to detect how conditions in the past banished certain individuals, things, or ideas, how circumstances rendered them marginal, excluded, or repressed. Sociology must preoccupy itself with what has been lost . . . the lost is only apparently absent because the forced 'disappearance' of aspects of the social continues to shadow all that remains. Because the past *always* haunts the present, sociology must imaginatively engage those apparitions, those ghosts that tie present subject to past histories."[3]

DEMONS

In addition to the spirits of the dead, Donna attracted the attention of demons as well, many of whom became alarmed by the new birth of a child of God. Yet she was tipped off about an impending demonic attack whenever her apartment looked "dark and grayish" in the spirit realm.

"The truth is," she observed, "that when you go into the spirit world, you never know what you're going to get into. You don't know what's going to come at you, what's going to jump on you. One night, I started to fall asleep, and all of a sudden, these skeleton figures just started coming out of doorways and everywhere, grabbing me, pulling my hair, hitting, cutting me with swords. They were like devil creatures, and they were moving really fast while they were attacking me. In the corner of my bedroom, I could see this big, big black-like shadow, and it wasn't moving, but I knew this shadow was controlling them and telling them what to do. And the whole time they were coming at me, I was not afraid. I was fighting as they were pulling me, clawing me, biting me. I'm telling them, 'I'm not afraid of you, I'm not afraid!' I just kept saying—'I'm not afraid of you!' I just kept saying it and fighting them at the same time. I went to sleep the next night, and they came at me again."

Demonic attacks became a regular occurrence in Donna's apartment the more she fought back. One time she awoke in the spirit realm, and to her surprise, there were what looked like demonic babies in her kitchen cabinets, "pulling stuff out. So, in that [spiritual] world, I took a red frying pan and started hitting the demons. There were three of them with fangs, and I was like, 'Get out of my house,' and they ran out of my front door," Donna sighed, shaking her head.

Unlike earthbound or unfamiliar spirits, demons had never lived in the flesh. Rather, they were created in hell with other devil creatures whose appearance was "enough to make you vomit," Donna emphasized, as we sat together on her couch. On this particular day, we were accompanied by her twenty-one-year-old granddaughter, Amber, whom Donna had recently begun training to enter the spirit world herself.

"Our sewer system ain't nothing compared to hell," Donna continued. "There are creatures who come from hell, and they stink. And demons stink, too. We might be sitting here watching TV, and we'll see a snake roll across the floor. We'll see some big old bug just crawling. Even my granddaughter, who is gifted like me, will see it. She'll say, 'Nana, you see that?' It's like these creatures keep fading in and out of this world. One minute, we'll see this world; the next minute, it's their world."

Donna's repeated contact with demons and hellish creatures affirmed the intimacy between the everyday and the ghostly. "This world here that we live in every day is somewhat by itself. However, these creatures can enter into this world. On the other hand, very few of us can choose to enter their world. But I do think that they create an imbalance by coming in and out of our world so often. Because it creates a situation in which people like me are living two separate lives. One minute we're here, the next minute we are there. One minute my granddaughter and I are sitting on this couch, and the next minute something sitting there with us."

"How does the enemy cross over into our world?" Donna asked me rhetorically, as she began to map the sacred geography of the spirit realm. "They come through portals, and I'm going to explain to you what a portal actually is, Onaje." She sat up on the edge of her seat.

"Grandma, let me explain," Amber interjected excitedly. "A portal is often a dirty area in the house. It usually smells, is filthy, and has bad odor."

"Yes, Amber," Donna smiled. "That's true, but portals are also pitch black."

"Yes, Grandma," continued Amber. "I was gonna say that it could be a corner of the room, and it can be very little, like a small circle or hole that something might pass through."

"That's true, Amber," Donna confirmed again. "It could be a pitch-black window, too. And you're right that you have to keep your house clean. If your house is filthy, the enemy will run rabid. And I've seen so many portals. Some demons are thirteen or fourteen feet tall, and they need portals so big that they are like doorways in the middle of a pitch-black hallway. When people go to the spirit world, they've got to be very, very careful where they're going, because these portals are dark and wide and tall, you know, and you be walking in the gates of hell and don't even realize it. And some people get so excited. They were like—'Yeah, I'm in the spirit world—da, da, da'—and then all of a sudden, you walking in the gates of hell, and no one realizes. Soon as I see dark, I'm like, get me out of here," she chuckled.

"One time, I was in the spirit world and I fell asleep, and in front of my bed, I saw this black door. And it was pitch black, and I could just tell it was a portal. The enemy can erect portals for itself. But like my granddaughter said, they will also look for cracks in your home, too."

Actually, it was through one of these overlooked cracks that demons first entered Donna's apartment in Roxbury. One evening she walked into her "living room, in the spirit world, and there could've been a good thirty of 'em in my house, just standing, gathering and talking, and congregating. I was like, 'What the heck is this? Oh, no!' And on the side of the wall over there, it looked like it was a little jukebox they got from somewhere and put it there to entertain themselves. That's why I say, they know how to take solid images from this world and bring it into that world. They also sometimes forget how to disconnect themselves from this world, so they could take this cup and bring it into the spirit world, thinking they're drinking from it. I'm telling you. Somewhere, they must've got a little jukebox. And it was playing music!"

WITCHCRAFT

In addition to demons, devil creatures, earthbound spirits, and unfamiliar spirits, there was a final category of beings that tested Donna's resolve to remain in the wilderness of the spirit realm: wizards and witches. Donna defined wizards and witches as living practitioners of esoteric arts who were able to move in and out of the spirit realm like her, but in their case, they did so on behalf of some evil end rather than in service of God's will.

One of Donna's first battles was with a wizard who was a shapeshifter and tried to frighten her into returning to her body from the spirit realm. This "evil priest come to me in the spirit. It came walking in wearing this black gown with an emblem on the front of it, and he looked like a wizard. He had a Mohawk, an earring coming from the side of his ear with a chain going into his nose, and I was in spirit, sitting on my bed. He just walked in the room, just kindly pulls up into the room," Donna rolled her eyes. "I looked at him and I'm like, 'What you gonna do?' He walks over to me and tries to scare me. His eyeballs come out of his eye sockets at me, and his mouth comes out of his jaw.

Everything's like, 'Pow,' like, freaky," she described. "I was like, 'That supposed to scare me?'" she asked the wizard in her street twang. "And then it just disappeared."

"Then there was another time, I kept having these visions of a woman with salt-and-pepper hair, and she had body parts all over her table—head, arm, leg, hand, everything. So I'm saying to myself, 'What?' I kept seeing this woman, kept seeing this woman, and I'm saying to myself, 'She gots to be a witch.' So the Holy Spirit keeps letting me see this person. So come to find out, she just keeps on trying to put some witchcraft on me. She just kept trying and trying and trying, and eventually she ended up giving up because she came to the realization that my power was coming from God. And once she realized that, she stepped off. I'm always coming up against someone who's dealing with witchcraft, and they're thinking they're so powerful that they can just knock me off the block. And they be bodacious about it."

Eventually there were so many witches, wizards, and other spirit creatures who were drawn into Donna's life and apartment that it pushed her deeper into the Word of God and her reliance on Jesus and the Holy Spirit for protection. This was how Donna first came up with the idea to turn her bedroom into a safe haven from the wilderness of the spirit world, much like the vacant apartment functioned at Columbia Point when she was a teenage girl. Not only did it become the place where she would frequently cross over into the spirit realm, but it was also where she returned to recharge her spirit and to resist evil through prayer, fasting, candle lighting, and reading the Bible. Having noticed this over time, Jesus and the Holy Spirit eventually formed a vibrational field of protection in front of her bedroom entrance.

"When I went to bed at night [and woke up in the spirit realm], I would see the Holy Spirit standing right at my bedroom door," affirmed Donna. "The Lord appeared to me when

I needed Him. The Lord was there. He was there. Before I would go to sleep in bed at night, He was always standing there. He never waved at me. He never said nothing. All He knew was that I just needed to see Him. He knew I just needed to see Him, and it was just enough for me." Tears began to roll down her face as she spoke. "And when I saw Him, it just made me dive into the Word of God. It made me worship more. It made me praise more. It made me keep my covenant more. It made me just keep going forward. It made me keep going toward my purpose and my destiny. It just pushed me every time, and He never gave up on me. And there's times when I was like, 'God, where you at? I'm going through this, where you at?' Praying and praying, waiting for a sign. I'm waiting for a flash of light to cross my ceiling. I'm just waiting for a sign, and then all of a sudden, I just stopped saying that, and I'm just like, silence. It's quiet. And all of a sudden, I *sense* that He's here. He's right with me."

The evening that Jesus and the Holy Spirit finally sealed Donna's bedroom permanently from evil, she awoke in the spirit world, only to realize that it was pitch black. "I was laying there in the bed, and I woke up in the spirit world, and it was dark. I knew it was dark. And when the enemy manipulates anything, it gets pitch black. The walls are so black that you couldn't even see your reflection in the mirror. But I knew that I was in my bedroom, and I heard the enemy howling like wolves, and then I heard them moaning and groaning. They were making noise like [groaning sounds], and you would be terrified, but I wasn't terrified, because as I lay there, I said, 'You can't do to me what you want to do to me,' and then the Holy Spirit appeared in my room. Jesus was standing in my bedroom door, and one hand was shielding me, and the other hand was shielding off my bedroom, and he wasn't saying nothing. Jesus wasn't saying anything. All I could feel is the shield coming over me. As I lay there, I could see this gold shield coming over me, and you could hear them hitting it, but I was feeling the vibration, but not the actual hit, and they were mad. They were heated! Those demons and spirits were heated that they could not get to me. They were trying to get me, and the Lord was stopping them. I finally made it so that they cannot enter my bedroom. My room is just locked down for evil. If they try to go, there's a force that's gonna stop them from coming in my room. I can see them outside my bedroom, and when I come out here in my living room, I'm open season for them. There's always going to be someone who's gonna come up and try to challenge me, and I'm not cocky. I'm not like, 'Oh, yeah, you.' No, my thing is, I'm a child of God, he has given me this gift. I am not gonna sit back and let you punk me. No, uh-uh. I'm not gonna sit and look at you and say, 'Get away, leave me alone.' They don't respond to that. You've gotta say, 'I command you to leave me in the name of Jesus. No weapon formed against me will prosper.' You have to say it over, and you've gotta believe what you're saying, because if you don't believe what you're saying, they're gonna know you ain't real," explained Donna adamantly. She had indeed found a refuge in the wilderness of the spirit world, and now, with the blessings of Jesus and the Holy Spirit, she hoped to serve as one of God's warrior prophets.

9

TREASURES FROM HEAVEN

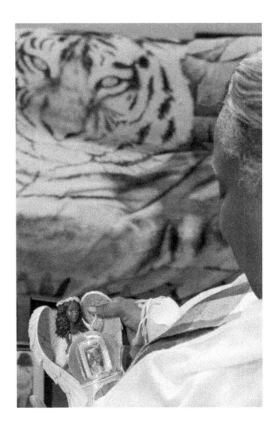

Donna was no longer a novice within the spirit world. Not only had she been tested by some of its worst inhabitants and classified them based on their relationship to the demonic, she had also learned how intertwined the spiritual realm is with the everyday life of her community.

Portals were everywhere, from a Roxbury courtroom or a grocery store to cracks in a floorboard or a dirty closet, and powerful spirits such as demons could erect gateways between the two worlds anywhere all by themselves. Some of them even attempted to take physical objects from her living room and other places into this immaterial zone, like an old cup or a jukebox playing their favorite tunes. Indeed, the two worlds were not separate at all but rather remained in constant intercourse, and Donna had negotiated the wilderness in between, as if the Holy Spirit was tutoring her soul to become a flash of grace through the darkness.

Sometime after she had demonstrated her unwavering commitment to serve as an emissary of Spirit, and her bedroom had been sealed off from demonic forces, Donna was surprised to receive other extraordinary gifts from the Holy Spirit, items she came to refer to as "treasures from heaven." These presents were in the form of supernatural powers, which some Christian Holiness traditions refer to as a "third work of grace," following rebirth and sanctification.[1]

The angel who announced the arrival of Donna's gifts floated into her bedroom one evening with the wings of a graceful fairy, wearing a dazzling gown made of gold with stardust sprinkled through her soft, flowing hair. She had a beauteous bag in her hand covered in splendid pinks, yellows, blues, and purples, with Hebrew letters scrolled across the sides.

"So I turned around, and I stand there, and she's smiling at me, so I knew she was good, and the bag looked like it was heavy," beamed Donna. "She said to me, 'These are the rest of your gifts.' So she handed me the bag, and when she handed me the bag, you would think it was heavy by the look of it, but it was as light as a feather," explained Donna, suggesting its immeasurable value.

"The next thing, you turn around, and she said, 'Use your gifts for good and not for evil.' She said to me, 'You have the ability to fly, to travel.'" Now Donna could enjoy the gift of tele-portation, the capacity to bounce to different spaces and times in order to positively affect the present. But she was never to use this power for personal gain at the expense of other people.

"She then brought me to Martin Luther King Boulevard from Washington and Dudley [in Roxbury]. I'm at the boulevard, and all the sudden, she took my hand, and I just went flying above the boulevard. I went to different realms of the universe and of heaven, and I met different people, and they're all telling me to use my gifts for good and not for evil."

As they traveled far distances, Donna and the stardust angel eventually landed on the corner of Longwood Avenue, near the entrance to Boston Children's Hospital. As the two of them stood there, behind the thin veil that camouflages the spirit world from ordinary sensory perception, they watched people come and go in the weekday afternoon hustle. Suddenly Donna saw that one of the young women walking toward her looked like her granddaughter, Amber, only much older, maybe in her mid-thirties, and wearing blue scrubs.

"And I yelled, I said, 'Amber!' and she's looking around" but couldn't see Donna.

As Donna watched her granddaughter walk toward the hos-pital entrance, she understood the lesson from the stardust angel right away. Her granddaughter would one day be employed in the medical field. Donna should use the gift of teleportation to see other people's pasts and futures to offer them guidance in the present. After she returned from her flight with the stardust angel, she contacted Amber and told her to pay attention to opportunities in the medical field.

"I didn't believe her," Amber explained to me about her grandmother's advice. But when I asked Amber what she did for work, she smiled and said, "Medical billing and coding."

Donna couldn't get enough of the thrill of flying. Of course, it took her a while to get over her fear of heights and the concern that, one day, she might not be able to return to her body after such a far-reaching zoom through the universe. But once she overcame her fear, Donna began to relish the weightlessness of being in the spirit realm, where she could leave her old self behind.

"I was flying in the clouds, like, 'Whoo, whoo!' One time, I was flying in my living room, flying around here in the room, in the spirit world. And now, I love it. It's a freedom. When you're traveling in the spirit world, it's such a freedom. It's a lightness, it's like everything that you're going through here doesn't go with you there. And it's like going into never-never land. You don't know what you're going to see, what you're going to hear, or who's going to speak to you, who's not going to speak to you. You just don't know. I mean, I remember one time I went into the cosmos! I literally went into the universe."

The evening she traveled into the universe on her own without the aid of the stardust angel was as unexpected as it was astounding to Donna, especially because she gained a new understanding of the true nature of space-time. On that evening, she explained, "I fell asleep, and I saw myself in the universe. I call it the universe because there were stars everywhere. And in space, there was a road, and on the road were images traveling, some going forward and others going backward. They weren't going up and down. They were going forward and backward. And they were passing each other, like time was passing by. I literally saw this man on the road of time. He looked just like the film character Edward Scissorhands. He was riding a bike with a hat on his head, and he just stared at me on his way down the road."

Donna realized intuitively that she was seeing space and time as a fabric of events that were occurring more slowly than she was, enabling her to view the past and future as an object in the distance. True to her calling as Child of Light, it was as if her ethereal self was moving through the cosmos at light speed, turning time into a slow-moving object relative to her own perspective. From the vantage point of the speed of light, Donna could enter the past or future in surprising ways, and always to make the present more livable for other people.

Donna began referring to these two modes of perceiving space-time, the one transcendent, the other mundane, as spiritual time and as time of the flesh.

"Now, when I close my eyes, and I read events in a person's life that haven't actually occurred yet, I know it's because the person has not caught up with [spiritual] time. You see, sometimes the flesh has not caught up with the spirit. Some people describe the experience as déjà vu, a feeling of having done something before. Well, your flesh hasn't caught up with what your spirit already knows. When I'm seeing the images coming to me, they're coming in and out, in and out of my consciousness, but a person's body may have not caught up with what I am seeing. When you're a prophet, you see the past, the present, and the future. It's so weird. And what's really weird, when I see the future, it is as if it is literally passing me by. It's like, He's letting me see it, but it goes by me. Why does it go by?" Donna asked me rhetorically, about the fabric of space-time, as we sat on her couch.

"I ask this question because I want to see if you are paying attention, Onaje," she laughed. "I'm seeing something from the future, but it goes by me, it goes by the present. Why? Now, I'm going to tell you why. Because it has to go into the future. And if I see something in the past, it has to literally travel backward into the past. When you're a prophet, you have to discern whether what you're seeing about someone deals with the past, present, or future. There are times I have caught myself, and I've said things to people, and they'll be like, 'No, this isn't happening in my life.' But then I realized—wait a minute, wait a minute, it hasn't happened yet. It hasn't happened *yet*."

THE GIFT OF SIGHT

In addition to teleportation, Donna learned that the stardust angel's bag also contained the power of sight into the other world. At first Donna's view into the spirit realm appeared as an array of "white lights coming around me," as she described it to her daughter Alexis one day.

"Mom, people who have cataracts have that!" Alexis replied with a worried look on her face.

"Alexis, I don't think they're cataracts," Donna laughed. "These white lights would just appear, when I walk, when I sit up, when I lay down. I would see a flash of light right here, a flash of light right there, little round white circles, and when I closed my eyes, I would see these little round white circles, and then when I'm walking."

Over time Donna realized that she was seeing the indwelling presence of the Holy Spirit in her mind as it guarded her aura from evil. "The white light that I'm seeing is the Lord protecting me when an enemy attacks me. Then, when they're really attacking me, I would see that light bounce right off of me. I literally see it right off of me, as plain as I'm sitting right here,

I would see the light just bounce. The light just ricochets off of me, that white light, and I started to see it," Donna stared off into the distance as if peering into its luminescence.

Eventually that light became Donna's window into the spirit world. "I learned to lay down awake and allow the visions and images to come to me," she revealed. "I have to be in calmness. I have to be laying down with my eyes closed, and I'll see a window, and then the next minute, I'm going into that window, and it just opens up. Now, there are times that I'm just out on the other side of that window, and I'll see motion. I'll see images of people and places. It's like I don't know. The best way I can describe it is from the movie *The Landers*, where these people get on a plane, and all of a sudden they wake up, and they're somewhere else, in a different universe or whatever. Once they finally figure out what's going on, they go back to the airport, and they sit up against a wall, and they literally see people coming in front of them from their universe of origin, and before you know it, these images of people close in until there's no separation between the two worlds. That's exactly how it is for me. I close my eyes, and I see the picture of things happening in the window. You just see the people walking and walking, and before you know it, 'Boom!' I'm right there."

There were other techniques Donna practiced in order to calm her mind enough to peer into the spirit realm, such as reading the Bible, praying, and listening to music in a contemplative manner. These spiritual disciplines helped her keep distracting thoughts at bay.

"What you got to do is go back to the beginning, where you came from in the Word of God. You got to start picking up that Bible. I read the Bible, but I pray more in the spirit. That Bible's right here next to me. It's right next to me. I'm back in the Word of God. I'm going back into the book like when I was three months into the Word of God. If I'm under a lot of stress, I regroup myself, make myself strong again and more in the spirit and not in the flesh. If you're going through financial problems, if you're going through relationships, or you're having problems with your kids or problems with your health, all that can be a distraction. But the Lord helps me by allowing the songs that play in my head to drown the voices out, to drown out the negative thoughts. I would hear a song playing in my head all day, and all night. I would wake up hearing it. I would go to sleep hearing it. The songs helped me drown them out. So all this is replacing others' thoughts with God's thoughts. He can't come in there with all that up in there. It's toxic. It's not toxic to the Holy Spirit, but it's toxic for the Child of God. So clean it out. It's like going in the ocean and just waving and swimming, and just like Moses parted the Red Sea, and you just keep pushing it aside and pushing it, and, 'Boom!'"

Through her prayers and a unique style of Christian meditation she created for herself, Donna slowly walked into her gift of spiritual vision.

"Now, sometimes when someone's living a busy life, sometimes when you pray, and you're trying to pray, you can't pray because there's so much chatter going on in your head. And then, when you try to pray, this thing pops up, that pops up. Oh my God. When I was clearing my mind for the first time to make it open for the Holy Spirit, every time, this thought would happen, that would happen. I was like, 'Wait a minute, hold up.' So what I did, I put the image of Jesus in my mind, me seeing Him for the first time, and I'd close my eyes, and I would just see Him standing there for the first time, and every time a negative thought came to my head, I would block it out with the vision of Jesus. I would literally relive that vision over and over again.

So, when you do this, all of a sudden, you can direct your inner voice [clearly] without distractions. For example, I'm saying to myself right now, 'I love you, Donna.' I'm saying to myself, 'Hey Donna, what's going on?' I'm saying all this right now, and there's nothing there [in my mind] but me. You've got to get to that level. And then, when that box is open, then you will be able to hear the voice of the Holy Spirit, only then. He can't come in there with all that chatter in there. How can He come in there when he's hearing this thought and that thought? How can He come in there when all that chatter going on in your head? And you've got people who have been in church for twenty years, fourteen years, ten years and haven't even heard the voice of the Lord because you've got so much going on in your head."

As Donna continued to develop her gift of sight into the other world, there came a point at which she realized that it was the Holy Spirit who opened and closed the window into the spirit world. In other words, she entered the other world only with the permission of the Holy Spirit, who functioned as gatekeeper of sorts between dimensions.

"When it is the Holy Spirit's will for me to see into the spirit world, it is as if He just takes His hand and waves it over my eyes, opening the gate to the other word. It's like a window. And it opens up and you just go, your spirit goes to the window, and it's like a window just opens up, and you'll see a square come down toward you, and then your spirit gravitates to the window and eventually you're inside. It's almost like I'm watching a movie, but the only thing is that I'm in the screen. It's like if I were to take me and put me in the screen, and that's how it is when I see things. When I first started to enter the window, I kept seeing these images, something flying up, down, wings flapping and stuff, and I couldn't see what it was. So I said to the

Holy Spirit, I said, 'Holy Spirit, I don't know what I'm seeing. If you allow me, Holy Spirit, to see because I don't understand what I'm seeing,' and He just took His hand and waved it, and I saw it. It was a battle."

To Donna's surprise, the Holy Spirit had allowed her to see spiritual warfare between angels and demons in the other world. No, Donna wasn't simply a prophet. She was a warrior too. "I saw javelins, balls of fire, and double-edged swords. I saw angels being wounded and other angels taking that angel away and ten more coming when one had gone. And I mean, God's angels were not backing down. They were not backing up. They were going right toward the enemy. No fear. I saw one angel, a big angel, big feathers, wings, and I was looking at it, and the Holy Spirit wanted me to see how the angel stood firm and didn't move, how it took his lumps but didn't move. And He said to me, 'This is who you are, my child.' This is why I say, I'm a warrior. I tell people that I'm a warrior. I don't have no time to dance with no demon. I don't got time to dance with no evil spirit. As soon as I sniff you, and you smell like you've got wickedness all over you, I'm gonna go pray. I'm gonna speak the powers of tongue. And the more He advances me up to the different levels, the more demons come around me. But St. Michael the Archangel is protecting me."

THE GIFT OF OTHER ANGELS

The stardust angel with the golden gown was not the only heavenly being to visit Donna and to support her advancement up the many levels of spiritual perfection. St. Michael, the warrior angel and defender of the Catholic Church against Satan, also visited her on occasion. After all, in Donna's eyes, becoming Baptist didn't exclude her from remaining Catholic. Other angels came to her, too, each of them reminding her to use her newly acquired gifts "for good and not for evil."

"I been told so many times that my angels love me, that they adore me. I've been told so many times, so many times. I remember when I had a vision, I saw an angel flying, and it looked like a white sheet flying through the universe. I was like, 'What is that?' I kept looking and looking and looking, and it was an angel. It was silky and beautiful. There's all types of angels, you know?" Donna observed, affirming that the universe was full of mystery and expansive enough to be populated with angels and spirit beings from several traditions.

As Donna gained further expertise in the spirit realm, she learned to differentiate between the types of angels who lived there. God had created some of the angels in heaven, she realized, while others "were people once living" whom God had transformed into angels because of their exemplary conduct on earth. Very rarely, though, did any of the angels look similar, and most did not have wings. In fact, they were often made from natural elements, such as stardust and gold, water, trees, and light. One angel in particular left Donna in a state of awe and wonder—especially given her kinship with fire.

"I saw an angel of fire walk across my floor. It was a male angel, and he smiled at me, and he was made out of fire. And it was so amazing! I was in the spirit world, in my living room, and when I saw him, I had to turn around. It was so amazing. It was like from the waist down this angel was all white. His foot was made out of white light, all this [his torso] was white light, right? Didn't look like he was wearing pants or nothing, just tippy-toeing across the floor [laughter]. And I stood there—I was amazed. His hands were like fire. And he had features of a human. I didn't say anything. I just stood there, and I heard him say, 'I'm here to protect you, my child.' And that was it."

Donna also relished in her visitations from St. Michael, whom she referred to as her chief guardian angel and protector.

"I saw him twice. The first time I saw St. Michael, the archangel, I was in a trance, and I fell asleep. I thought I was awake, but I was in the spirit world. I go in that world so fast. I literally saw him battling a demon right above me that was coming to attack me. And I looked up, and I literally saw him battling this demon. Do you hear me? I was so scared. I thought—I'm lying in the spirit world with my eyes closed—my eyes closed tight. I was like maybe I wasn't supposed to see him, but I saw him. He had his armor on just the way we see pictures of him. His wings, everything."

The second time Donna saw St. Michael, it was in the evening while she was flying throughout the cosmos. "One night, I was in the spirit world, and I said, 'Jesus, I love you,' and my spirit was floating all around in the universe just flowing all around, and as I was levitating up, I see something descending down to me. As it became closer to me, something said to me, 'Take its hand,' and I extend my hand, and I take his hand, and I see it's St. Michael the Archangel, and he says, 'I'm here to protect you my child,' and that's it."

In addition to St. Michael, one of the most important angels Donna became aware of was the one she referred to as the Hummingbird. Rather than working alongside her, however, the Hummingbird performed her wonders by taking possession of her body and vocal cords, turning the sound of Donna's voice into a spiritual weapon.

"I have this spirit that's with me. Her name is the Hummingbird. One day I'm sitting here, and all the sudden I start to

sound like I'm an opera singer, singing real opera. So I'm singing, I'm just singing opera, and out of nowhere angels are just
coming out of everywhere, and the Hummingbird, she's singing, and she's singing through me. It's my voice, and I can hear
my voice, but she's singing through me, and I look all around
my living room, and angels are just everywhere, and they're listening to her. They're listening to her. She is like the most
ultimate—when she comes, it's over. When she comes, it's over
for the enemy. Any demon, any evil spirit, any evil creature, it's
over, and I think that when she sings, she gives messages to God's
angels, and so many arrive, and they're beautiful. These angels
do have huge wings."

THE GIFT OF ANCESTORS

In addition to angels and winged messenger spirits, Donna
received other spiritual companions as she grew in her power, in
the form of African and Afro-Jamaican ancestor spirits. As she
floated out of her bedroom and into her living room one evening,
Donna realized she had just interrupted some sort of African gala
event being held among ancestral spirits in her sitting area. One
woman impressed Donna the most. She found "this African
lady sitting on the couch. She had a dashiki, a turban on her
head, scars on her face, and she was big. She was a big lady. She
smiled, had beautiful big eyes, and I was like, 'Wow,' and I was
happy, because I knew they've got a message for me. I'm excited.
So I walked over to the couch, and I stand over there, and she's
sitting there. She turns around, and she looks at me, and when
she opens her mouth, the reaction I got, I was like, 'Hold up,
lady!' She said to me, 'What are you gonna do with the money?'
She caught me off guard. I was like, 'I don't know, I'm gonna

help my family. I'm gonna help my family.' She just turned around and said that to me. And all the rest of them are just standing there looking at me, stone-faced. They ain't saying nothing, so she's the leader. But they were all African, and I was like, 'Wow.'"

Sometime afterward, Donna found herself on the ground in the spirit realm burning up from a source of heat she could not see. As she lay on the floor on her knees, she squinted her eyes and saw only "these white feet going around me in a circle, and each of them are touching me, and every time someone touched me, I'd go, 'Ah,' and I'm just going deeper into the spirit."

Eventually Donna realized that she was being initiated into the spiritual community of her African ancestors. "I took on their characteristics. Whatever abilities they have, entered me. I am strong willed and opinionated because that is how they were when they were living. And God assigned them to me to teach me. God felt that they would honor Him and protect me," she revealed. And once they had finished the ceremony, they, too, turned to Donna and implored her to use her gifts for good and not for evil.

"Onaje," Donna reminded me as she discussed her African past, "you and I share the same African ancestors. I have thirteen who are always around to me. The ancestors around you are also African."

I smiled.

THE GIFT OF TONGUES

Donna's gift of divine speech developed after her first chemo treatment for breast cancer but continued to evolve, especially whenever she was feeling ill.

"I got the gift of tongues when I had my first chemo treatment. The tongues came over me," she reminisced. Allowing the Holy Spirit to speak through her in indecipherable sound fragments had the effect of not only warding off evil but also of rejuvenating her body, it seemed. It happened again several years after her cancer went into remission, when Donna suffered a series of life-threatening asthma attacks stemming from smoke inhalation in the house fire as a child. Since she couldn't physically speak during one of these asthma attacks, she discovered that she had been given the ability to speak "tongues" telepathically in her mind.

"This was the most amazing thing. I started speaking tongues in my thoughts. I never knew how, didn't know. I'm lying in my bed, I'm afflicted with illness, and I'm having a lot of asthma attacks, and I can't leave the house, and I'm lying in the bed and just praying, and all of a sudden I hear my tongues playing in my head. And literally, once I caught on to it, I was like, 'Yeah!' [Laughter] I was like, 'Yeah, I can do tongues in my thoughts!' So, I'm literally hearing the tongues in my head, and I'm letting it play over and over again. I lay there for two hours. Once someone learns to speak tongues and the spirit of the Lord comes over you, let it flow. Don't stop."

One afternoon Donna also found herself speaking tongues that sounded like a foreign language. As she cleaned the rug in her living room, she suddenly sensed evil and incarnated the Holy Spirit while her body continued to roll the vacuum across the floor. As she fought in the other world, Donna's tongues erupted from her mouth, which, to her surprise, sounded like Chinese. Jason, who happened to be spending time in Donna's apartment, was using the bathroom when he heard Mandarin-like speech coming from the living room.

"Donna, did you know that you were speaking Chinese?" Jason asked surprised, when he came out of the bathroom.

"That's when my Chinese tongue came out," said Donna with a smile.

As with all her gifts, Donna had to discern when it was appropriate to use her tongues for good and not evil given the power of sacred speech to materialize things into being.

"If I speak what I'm feeling, it will come to life. So I have to speak life over someone," she explained. "And if I am disappointed in someone, I silence my tongue, because I know when I speak life, if I say 'You're gonna get a job next week,' it's gonna come to pass. It will come to pass. But if I'm disappointed in someone or someone displeases me, no! I won't even vent. I won't open my mouth. I will be silent the whole time," she related, before stopping in midspeech as if she was suddenly touched the spirit.

"Thank you, Holy Spirit," she exclaimed as we sat on her couch. "I see my light all the time now. It's just always here, ricocheting out. As I'm speaking to you, the light ricochets off of me."

GIFT OF DISCERNMENT

Donna eventually began to understand what her spiritual companions meant when they implored her to user her gifts for good and not evil. Essentially, it meant that Donna was to discern whether the use of her gifts would contribute to the greatest good of the communities she was being prepared to serve.

"I had to figure it out for myself, and I finally realized the meaning. When you're gonna help prophesy to someone, the information you give them must have a good outcome. It can't just have good intentions," she explained.

For this reason, Donna sometimes refused to use her prophetic gifts, even when asked to by close friends and people suffering from emotional pain.

"A friend of mine, her son had lost someone close to them. They called me, wanting to know the people that did it and names, and I automatically said, 'No,' and the thought came in my head, 'You should do it for good and not for evil,' and that's when I knew what it meant. Another time, this woman came to me. Her boyfriend was cheating on her. She wanted to know the address to the girl's house, her description and everything. I could see the description, I knew where their house was, but I wasn't giving her jack, and she's like, 'Well, I thought you was supposed to—' I said, 'No, you gonna beat up that girl, and you gonna use my gift to do it? No, I'm not gonna let you do it. I'm not gonna let you do it.' And sometimes, when someone's really, really grieving for someone, I will see their deceased loved ones spirit, but if I see that person's grief is really bad, I'm not gonna let that person know that I see their loved one and allow them to go through that grieving process again, because if they're not strong enough to handle what I have to say, then it's not right to tell. I just can't be all, 'Your son's talking to me,' or 'Your daughter's talking to me,' or 'Your mom's talking to me,' or 'Your dad's talking to me.' I can't do that," declared Donna.

There were some occasions, however, when Donna was in doubt about whether a course of action would lead to a positive outcome, and in those moments, she would often rely on angels who would appear and offer her reassurance. "It's true what the scripture says—His thoughts are higher than our thoughts—that He hears our thoughts.[2] As soon the thought comes to me, there's the angel shoving it out, telling me not to worry. Don't worry. Everything's going to be all right. Giving me reassurance. Because that's how much He's invested in me."

In addition to developing her ability to discern when to use her gifts, Donna also had to learn subtle ways of distinguishing angels from demons in the spirit realm, lest her prophetic gifts be easily manipulated. One sure way to do so, she discovered, was to notice how much the spirit being talked to her.

"Angels don't converse with you," she observed. "When I first saw the angel give me my gifts, she didn't have a whole lengthy conversation with me. This is for a reason. Whenever the angels speak to me and communicate with me, they say, 'We're not here to tell you what to do or how to do or when to do it. We're here to guide you. We're here to protect you,'" revealed Donna, as if to suggest that angels (unlike demons) live by a code of ethics in the spirit world designed to protect each human being's agency and free will.

"They're not allowed to talk with you unless the Holy Spirit gives them permission to talk to you. And these rules are in place in order to protect you. The angels watch you and are there to protect you. They will only speak to you when the Holy Spirit allows them to speak to you. So that is a lesson right there for you, Onaje." Donna looked at me with the patience of a wise teacher. "If all of a sudden you think you see an angel, but it starts speaking to you, that's when you need to be concerned. Now, if they [angels] sense that you want to communicate with them, they're going to make that possible for you. But it won't be exactly in the form of communication we have in this world. They cannot communicate with you that way. So I knew early on that whenever a spirit talks too much, it is evil. Some people might say how do you know the devil, the enemy Satan? Well, because the angels told me what to expect from early on. So I picked up on that immediately, and whenever I hear something that sounds like gossip, I automatically know that it is evil spirits, demons, or unclean spirits, trying to manipulate," Donna explained.

"I automatically know who they are because demons run their mouths. They want to communicate with you. They want to talk with you, and sometimes they can't really talk the way we talk without having a raspy voice. Evils are gossips, and they're snitches. They're telling on each other. They have conversations with you. They call you by your name. They talk too much. See, the Bible says, 'Trust the Lord and do not lean on your understanding.'[3] It is the whole sole purpose of Satan to win your trust, so they've got to run their mouth to get you to trust them and to trust the flesh. So that's how they come at God's children."

Donna wanted to offer me a concrete example of how an unfamiliar spirit attempted to interfere with her free will.

"One day I was opening my window, or closing my window, and I heard a voice say to me, 'Be careful. You're gonna fall.' And I said, 'Wait a minute. Ain't no angel gonna say that to me, and immediately, I'm gonna rebuke you in the name of Jesus.' I immediately said that. And then I knew that it had to be an unclean spirit. I knew it because I kept sensing that this spirit was talking to me too much, responding to my every thought and my every need, and I was like, that don't sound right. So I went in my room. I closed my door, and I went onto the bed, and I went straight into the spirit world. The fact that I was deceived, I was pissed off that I got deceived. I was like, oh, no. I was in there, and I was all over my bedroom [fighting that unclean spirit]. My family who was in the living room was like, 'Donna, boy, that must have been a battle up in there!'" she chuckled. "These demonic spirits try to come to me and gangster me and I ain't playing that!"

Over time, Donna discerned how use demonic gossip against those manipulative beings. If, for instance, she was prophesying to someone and wanted to know the origins of that person's problems, she would listen closely to the demons chattering around that individual. Often demons didn't realize she could hear them, and in their displays of arrogance, they would discuss how they were afflicting their host. Once Donna had heard enough, she would surprise them by speaking directly to them in front of their afflicted host, telling them to "shut-up and leave my presence in the name of Jesus. When evil tries to come at me, my skin starts to itch. I start to break out with hives, as if I have allergies," she shivered.

THE GIFT OF PROPHECY

Seeing into the past, present, and future of an individual required Donna to pay close attention to the angels, demons, and other spirits surrounding them. She adamantly rejected the idea that she was a mind reader or a possessor of psychic abilities.

"People often say to me, 'How do you know these things?' I spoke to someone the other day, and I said, 'You're thinking about taking a trip.' I said, 'You're gonna take that trip,' and she said, 'How did you know I was going to Disney World?' And some people will ask, 'What, are you reading my mind?' I'm not reading your mind," Donna insisted. Rather, she suggests, it is the Holy Spirit who knows each individual's mind and, because it indwells within her, the Holy Spirit delivers that information so that she might serve as its messenger.

"The only one that can read your mind is the Holy Spirit, and I am that close to it that it will transcend such information to me," she suggested, affirming that hers is a spirituality of consciousness. And of course, Donna does not always share everything the Holy Spirit reveals. "And there's a lot of things I don't tell because it's not for this time, and my tongue is tied. The Holy Spirit shows it to me, and I leave it at that."

Given that Donna's knowledge comes from the Holy Spirit, she believes that her correct title is that of prophet, even if there are those in the church who don't think a Black woman who has had an abortion and lives in poverty is holy enough to embody God's Word.

"I believe the correct title for me is prophet. But no one is ever ready to receive me as a prophet. When I determined that I was a prophet, other people laughed. I guess they assumed that a person had to reach a certain level of holiness to be a prophet. But if the Holy Spirit feels that I have reached an appropriate level of holiness, who am I to question Him?" Donna asked. "Why should I accept what people are saying over what the Holy Spirit has given me and what I'm experiencing?"

Donna lived her religion outside the bounds of the church and the authority of recognized religious experts. And she applied the same logic to her ability to bless holy water and oil for the protection and healing of others. Why couldn't a black woman from the projects turn water holy? she asked.

"My mother would send me to church to get holy water, and now I said to myself, what does it mean to be holy? Maybe I can bless water, so I blessed water. I found out I have the gift to bless water. I make up holy oil as well. Let me bless holy oil. I sit at my table and bless the oil. I put my hand on the oil, and I close my eyes, and I pray, and the oil becomes holy. I start rubbing it in the areas of affliction on my body or the bodies of others. The pain goes away," she declared as she showed me how holy oil was meant to seal and protect the human body's spiritual gateways.

"You put it on your arm here like this. Right here, on your forehead. Then go like this to your head [Donna makes a cross on my forehead]. These are the gateways where the enemy tries to come into your flesh. They try to come into your head. They try to come into your throat and right here in the back of your neck. And through here. So what you do, you close the doors to them. I found out that God gave me the ability to bless water and to bless oil, and I never knew that I was gonna have the ability until I did it."

A WARRIOR PROPHET BORN

Donna had been granted her diploma from heaven, emerging as a resourceful warrior prophet with the gifts of teleportation, visions, light projection, guardian angels, ancestors, tongues, prophecy, and ethical discernment. After almost five decades negotiating the structural inequities of Boston, she had become more at home in the spirit world than she was in the city. To her, the physical side of reality was likened to a cocoon, a chrysalis, which circumscribed her identity narrowly within the darkened regions of other people's minds. The glistening butterfly of her new consciousness had emerged stunningly from those confines, in order to float to other worlds on the wings of the Holy Spirit as only the oppressed have imagined in their dreams.[4]

"I've felt like I am living in a cocoon, knowing that I have these abilities, knowing that He keeps blessing me, but also recognizing that people don't understand. And even now, just recently, this morning, I heard the angels saying to me that you are going to be blessed, that you're going to have a blessing. And they were praising me, everything I'm doing with offering my story to you, Onaje, they were saying that it's gonna help people, telling me it's gonna help people, that the Lord has favor for me. But I don't know what I'm gonna do from one moment to the next. I don't know what ability I'm gonna have. It just keeps escalating."

10

THE DEVIL IS A LIAR

I t had been years since the day Jason introduced me to Donna, during which time she had become an extraordinary figure in my life. Being in her presence for so many hours, watching her interact with unseen ghosts, laughing at her bodacious wit, and being nurtured by her selfless love had changed me in ways that I never could have anticipated. For one, I came to understand how much gender-based evil I had overlooked, hidden away, or otherwise learned to ignore in the world. The images of Black women as jezebels, "the ultimate mammy, the emasculating bitch, the tragic mulatta, the castrating matriarch, and the pickaninny" were no longer abstract ideas for me but registered in the scarring of the flesh of Donna, the very person whom I had come to regard as a mother.[1]

One wintery afternoon, wading in the painful awareness of Donna's lifelong suffering, I felt forced, almost compelled, to visit the memorial site of Phillis Wheatley, a Senegalese woman who was enslaved in Boston in 1761 and was the first Black person in the American colonies to publish a book of poetry. As I walked down Boston's Commonwealth Avenue, I imagined Wheatley's unbearable suffering during the Middle Passage of the transatlantic slave trade. She had been torn completely from her roots as a little girl and encountered the painful lash of the whip, the likely sexual exploitation of her body, and the relegation her humanity to the status of a thing.

Then, in the distance along Commonwealth Avenue, I suddenly saw her memorial statue come into view—her elegant bronze body leaning over a stone tablet, a quill pen in her right hand, her left hand touching her cheek in quiet contemplation—and without warning a well of grief overcame me, and I began to cry uncontrollably in the middle of the road. "My mother, my mother," I sobbed as I reached her memorial, speaking out loud as tears rolling down my face, despite the young man on a bench watching me with a perplexed look on his face in the distance. "I am so sorry you went through so much suffering! I am sorry that you were alone in Boston. I am sorry that they did this to you and treated you like an animal and tore you from your family!"

I leaned over her stone tablet with both of my hands, overcome by images of Phillis as a little girl, frightened in the hands of her masters. "I'm here for you Mom. I'm here for you," I cried, feeling in her the presence of a mom. "Your suffering did not go in vain. I promise to finish Donna's book for you. To tell her story is to tell yours. You both survived the unspeakable in Boston, separated by nearly 250 years. I love you Mom."

It was now raining. As drops of water slowly drizzled onto Phillis's face, it occurred to me that I had nothing to offer her as a gift. "Water" suddenly came to mind. I opened the water bottle I had been carrying in my jacket pocket and poured the smooth droplets onto the stone table in front of her as I prayed. "Mom, may you be at peace in the home of the ancestors, your pain washed away. May you go home, free from the chains of your past. May you know healing and freedom."

After the last droplet of water had washed across her memorial, I lifted my face, wiped away tears, and took one last look at her, before walking toward Massachusetts Avenue with a strange but palpable feeling of inner peace after having released so much pain. I had not expected to feel such deep emotions in the presence of Wheatley's memorial. And as I walked away, it became clear to me that Donna had changed me forever, an awareness of the evils haunting Black women in America making an indelible mark on my soul.

A few days later, while sitting in Donna's apartment, I told her that I was going to include Phillis Wheatley's poem *On Imagination* at the beginning of the book. Donna looked up at me and said in a matter-of-fact way, "Onaje, she's right there, sitting next to you on the couch. She's happy you're putting her in the book." My heart soared.

THE WAR BEGINS

Donna was at the pinnacle of her abilities and prepared to use her gifts on behalf of those living at the bottom of American society. At the height of her powers, she had turned the sanctuary of her bedroom into a "war room," with a special worship altar adorned with items she said held immense power. Whenever Donna sensed the need to transcend the limitations of her body, she retreated into this site of resistance and entered the spirit world. Sometimes she spent several days at her altar arming herself for battle, incorporating the tools of fasting and prayer, and the radiating flame of a candle.

"When you are battling a demon, don't go unprepared," she warned. "Always prepare yourself by praying and fasting before you do that divine intervention. Don't go blindsided. Because you will be blindsided, okay?" she asked me, turning her eyebrows up, before moving her attention to the Holy Spirit, whose presence she suddenly felt.

"I always—Thank you Holy Spirit," she uttered.

Donna never shared with me the full contents of her war room. She did, however, show me one powerful item. "The Holy Spirit wants you to see this," Donna revealed, as she walked into her bedroom and returned with something in her hand. "He wants it to be in the book." In her hand she held a large, clear glass bottle with a black cross drawn across the side. And inside the bottle stood the long wick of a candle, which remained erect and upright, even though the wax around it had long burned away. As I stared at the burnt candle's empty glass frame with its wick still intact, I realized that this object was a spiritual metaphor of Donna herself, designed to communicate something important about her identity in the spirit world. The wick was a representation of the nature of Donna's enduring soul, which, unlike the wax (her flesh), was impervious to the lethal flames of her environment. In other words, the candle stood for the special little girl who survived the housefire.

DEFEATING SEXUAL PREDATORS

Now that she was spiritually mature, one of Donna's most important assignments was to use her gifts to prevent sexual violence and other forms of brutality against women and children. Initially, Donna was just there to observe, like the time she teleported through the spirit realm to witness the murder of a young woman who was lying naked in bed at a remote cabin somewhere in the United States. "The Holy Spirit will let me just get closer and closer to it, and I will see it. So, as I'm looking and I'm hovering over this place, I see that it's a cabin. This woman's laying in the bed. She's under the blanket. She has no clothes on. The man comes into the cabin, and she's waiting for him, so you're thinking, okay. And you could see animals on the walls stuffed, like he's a hunter. The next thing, he turns around, he takes a pillow and smothers the woman. He kills her. And then he takes her, wraps her up in a sheet, takes her and buries her on the outside of his house." When Donna returned to her body in the physical world, she was stunned by what she had just witnessed.

On another occasion, Donna turned on her television, only to hear news about a young girl who had recently been murdered in Boston. All of a sudden, Donna explained, "[I] started getting images in my head, and I'm holding my head like this, and I'm like, hitting my head trying to stop these images, and all of a sudden, I see this girl opening her door, and this person starts shooting her. I never saw the face. I just see her being hit, and I see where she gets hit first on her body, and she falls to the floor, and she's trying to run from this person. When she opens the door, she doesn't know the person. Her look is like, 'Who are you?' And he pushes his way into her house. And this is what I see. And I was like, wow. I said to myself, wow." In this instance, rather than teleporting to some unknown location in the present, the Holy Spirit bounced Donna back in time to observe a stranger murder a young Boston woman.

On another occasion, Donna witnessed a girl in an undisclosed location getting "on an elevator, and the elevator door was gonna close, and just before the door was gonna close, someone came in the elevator. As soon as he came in the elevator, he snatched the girl, pulled a gun out, and shot the girl in the elevator. And I said, I used to say to myself, 'Lord, Father, why do I see so much violence?'" It took a while, but Donna finally got the message. The Holy Spirit wanted her to understand how thoroughly hatred against women is sewn into the cultural fabric of American society.

Sometimes the Holy Spirit also permitted Donna to intervene and prevent acts of violence against women and children. On one occasion she entered the spirit realm and suddenly teleported to a dangerous woman's house who was using her own children to lure unsuspecting kids into her home. "That's why I say sometimes the Holy Spirit will use you to go there, so this was one of His incidents where he used me," revealed Donna. As she floated above the woman's house in the spirit realm, she could see "kids riding a bike, and the kids in the yard, and there was a white house, and then the kids, the little kids, the woman's sons are calling this little boy to come into the house. The woman, I could see her standing in the door, and you could see that she's a witch. I told the little boy 'Don't go over, don't go in the house,' and he gets scared, and he gets back on his bike, and he runs," noted

Donna, this time using her telepathic powers to compel this little boy to escape harm.

"I said, 'Don't go over there. Don't go in that house. You will never see your mother and father again.' So the boy runs, and the woman, she gets mad at me and hisses at me. She doesn't say nothing, and I could tell she's a witch. And she gets mad because I stopped her [from kidnapping the little boy]."

As Donna entered the spirit world more frequently, exercising her own version of liberation theology in action, she also noticed an increase in the volume of demonic attacks on herself and the youngest girls in her immediate family. Since she had reached a certain level of spiritual maturity, demons were attacking her indirectly through her close relatives. Donna referred to these attacks as "generational curses," when trauma is transmitted intergenerationally within a single family. "You see, when something does something to you, if you got a strong spirit, it will go to whoever's closest to you and weak. It will bounce off of you, and it will go to them. I call them generational curses. That's what I call generational curses," she explained.

Donna discovered a generational curse afflicting her close relative Alecia. Alecia anxiously approached her one day with a horrible story. Every night she went to sleep, a man climbed into her bed to touch her private parts. Donna was furious. To be sure, she pulled Alecia aside to ask whether this man was a living human being or a spirit.

"He's a spirit," responded Alecia. Donna promised her traumatized relative in no uncertain terms that she would spend the night with her and confront this pedophile face-to-face.

So the following evening, after spending several hours arming herself in her war room in Roxbury, Donna showed up at Alecia's apartment, equipped with holy water and various oils, which she proceeded to splash across Alecia's bedroom door to create an impenetrable vibrational shield. "So I go in the house, and I put holy water all over the house. I drown Alecia's room so much, the walls were weeping holy water, oils. I put a shield outside the bedroom door so that it could not come near her. Then I deliberately stood guard over her house that night, deliberately," Donna said defiantly.

With everyone in the apartment was asleep, Donna lay in wait on the living room couch, like a seasoned hunter, poised to snare her prey.

"I'm going to get this thing," she mumbled to herself as she lit a match and placed the flame to a leaf of sage and allowed the pungent smoke to waft through the air.

Donna then turned to her Bible, prayed, and read the scriptures, "like I always do before I fall asleep. I knew it was watching me the whole time," she revealed, "but I let this thing think that I didn't see it at all. I didn't tip my hand yet. So I lay down in that living room, and I asked the Holy Spirit, 'Lord, take me there, take me. I want to go to the world, to the spirit world.' And as soon as I walked into the spirit world, that bad boy appeared, soon as I walked in there, and I saw him, and he literally leaned over me, and I jumped up off that couch so fast! I said to him, 'Didn't I tell you I was gonna get you?' And he was a white male pedophile. He was telling me how my granddaughter's going to be his. And that she belonged to him and this and that, right?" Donna asked, while also pointing out that the souls of the pedophile's parents were in the apartment too, watching her go to blows with their son from the sidelines. "And his parents were sitting in the spirit world on some banisters watching the whole thing in horror, and they did this scream at him, because they were angry with him and they were tormenting him."

As Donna brawled all over the living room with the pedophile, suddenly a throng of young white girls appeared in the room, all of whom had been raped and murdered by him.

"All the girls he had molested and killed appeared. Alecia's living room was literally full of them. And they saw me defeating this man, and they saw me defeating him. They just appeared out of nowhere. They was like all over the room. And his parents looked like they were Christians, because they were tormenting him. And they did some type of scream, they would go like this on his ears [thrust their mouths], and he put his hands over his ears so he couldn't hear what they were saying."

Donna's brawl with the pedophile must have been a harrowing experience. There she was, a poor Black woman from Roxbury, wrestling a white male pedophile in front of the girls whose lives he destroyed, with his parents there to observe. Those innocent little girls rooted for Donna with all their fieriness as her spirit smoldered with light, and with one last hurl, she finally launched the thug into nonbeing. Then, remarkably, after the pedophile vanished, his absence seemed to release the girls from the darkness of his torment. One by one, each of their sparkling souls moved into the light. Donna watched in awe.

"The Lord let me go over there to defeat him. And as soon as he got defeated, all the children's souls he tormented went from dark to light. And they went to Heaven," Donna smiled.

THE PEDOPHILE WITH DREADLOCKS

Donna was called on to defend other girls in her family from supernatural sexists as well. One night when her relative Zora was staying at Donna's apartment, Zora felt a man sneak up from behind her to touch her private parts.

"He tried to come up behind Zora. And I kept saying to myself—I kept walking around, and I said—'You just wait, I'm going to get you. You just wait, you just wait.'"

Donna retreated to her war room and prayed for the Holy Spirit to allow her to enter the gates of the spirit world. "I can only go in the spirit world when God allows me to go. I just can't go there on my own. He will allow that to happen. And I kept saying—'You just wait till the Holy Spirit lets me go there. I'm going to get you, buddy.' I sure did. I kept saying, and I kept saying it, saying it, saying it. I said—'I'm going to tell you, leave my Zora alone. Stay away from her,'" Donna repeated in her war room. Closing her eyes, Donna suddenly found herself in the other world, unbeknownst to this unfamiliar spirit.

"He thought he was so slick. He thought he was going to come from behind and surprise me, but I had already entered the spirit world," Donna revealed. When Donna walked into her living room, the pedophile "looked at me dead in my eye, looked surprised that I saw him. I took his dreadlocks, and I threw him [across the room], and there was another person with him, a little boy was no more taller than this [raises her hand waist-high]. The little boy was scared to death seeing me come at them. 'You think I can't see you?' I said. And the whole time that I had been seeing the spirit on the floor, he's not saying nothing to me. I said, 'Didn't I tell you you'll get yours? Didn't I tell you you'd get yours?' I said, 'Didn't I tell you to stay away from Zora?' I said, 'The next time I come at you, God will destroy you. And it's going to be God's will that I destroy you.' I said, 'So now you see, I can come. I definitely did come here to the spirit world!' They don't know how I do it, because I'm very much alive in the flesh," jeered Donna.

PROPHETIC IMAGINATION

In addition to her war against sexual violence, Donna also traveled through space-time to bring back precious information for her marginalized neighbors in Roxbury. Donna's prophetic gifts often showed up in the course of her ordinary day, as she went grocery shopping, had lunch at a corner deli, or rode public transportation through Boston's streets. More often than not, in these public spaces, she would come across Black women carrying the weight of the world on their shoulders. In those moments, Donna often knew right away, since the Holy Spirit would allow her to feel the woman's pain in her own body.

This was especially the case for an older Black woman Donna saw one day sitting on a bench inside the Stop and Shop grocery store on Blue Hill Avenue.

"Excuse me, mam," she said politely, as she felt in her bones that the woman was going through cancer treatment. "Can I sit next to you for a minute?"

"Yes, you may," said the woman looking up at her with a weary expression on her wrinkled face.

"The Holy Spirit brought me here today to tell you that this is your last battle with cancer. You won't have to deal with cancer anymore," Donna looked calmly into the woman's eyes. The woman on the bench reacted suddenly, by sobbing and thrusting her body into Donna's arms, tears running down her cheeks.

"It's okay, honey. I know you're tired. Everything is going to be okay," Donna consoled her, while shoppers looked on with bewilderment at the older woman crying in her arms.

After a few moments, Donna reached into her grocery bag and brought out a white candle. "The Holy Spirit told me to give you this candle," she said. "Light it and pray."

"You're an angel of God. You're an angel of God. You're an angel in the flesh," exclaimed the woman. "Thank you. Thank you," she cried.

"No, don't thank me," said Donna. "Thank God."

Suddenly the older woman's husband returned from shopping with a stern look of disapproval on his face. Donna knew intuitively that he did not support their interaction. It was as if he wanted to say to Donna, "Stop giving my wife false hope." Nevertheless, Donna ignored him and smiled at the older woman, who stood up as if she felt rejuvenated.

"I will see you again," predicted Donna. "And you will tell me what I said was true. That was God's will and God's timing," she said, and sure enough, years later, she did see the older woman. "And she was cancer free," beamed Donna.

Donna shared that feeling someone else's pain and knowing their thoughts was one of the most difficult aspects of being a prophet. "It's like putting on someone else's cologne or perfume. The aroma stays with you, and it's difficult to shake it off. I learned to do it eventually. I call it separation, disconnecting myself from a person I have just prophesied to. I learned how to let it go, to disconnect, because if not, I carry it around all day, and it will make me cry."

Donna's ability to carry other people's pain became real for me when I saw her prophesy to the mother of my childhood best friend, the one who died when I was a teenager. As the three of us casually chatted in a Thai food restaurant near Boston University eating tasty pad see noodles and crispy chicken, Donna suddenly interrupted the conversation.

"I'm sorry, honey," she said to my best friend's mother, apparently overwhelmed by the presence of her son's spirit. "But your son is here. He keeps saying to me, 'Tell my mother she has to live her life. She has to live her life,'" stressed

Donna. "He is saying it's okay to think about him, and to remember, but remember the good times, and you have to live, honey."

Tears began to roll down my best friend's mother's face. "I'm sorry to bring this up now," Donna apologized, "but he needed for you to hear this." As my friend's mother cried, I attempted to comfort her, knowing how much she needed to express her deeply held pain. And I looked over to Donna in amazement. This time, rather than extracting information from the future to bring back a cure for a Black woman in Roxbury, Donna had allowed the dead to speak from the past.

Donna's prophetic imagination also required her to teleport to future worlds across time-space for the benefit of Roxbury's forgotten women and children. One of the most remarkable examples of this occurred in the service of her close friend Angela. Angela called one evening to ask whether Donna had an extra padlock she could borrow to secure her suitcase during an upcoming trip to Cuba.

"Sorry, I don't," Donna explained. The two friends hung up just as Donna drifted off to sleep. "But when I went to sleep," she explained, "when I closed my eyes, and I open up, I was in the spirit world, so it was that fast. So I said okay, I'm in the spirit world. I come out, I walk out of my room, I'm in the spirit world, but in my room. I walk out in the living room, and I see things that you would have if you owned a nail salon. There were these three tables right near my door, and it looked like nail salons. I was like, what does this mean?" Donna asked herself, drawing on her gifts of discernment to understand the symbolic significance of the manicure tables.

"They [Holy Spirit and angels] were trying to tell me something, but I couldn't, I didn't really catch it when I saw the nails, the tables with the nails and perfumes, and all that stuff.

So then, when I saw the furniture, I said, oh, this is Angela's house. This is about Angela. It's not about me."

Donna was then bounced to Angela's apartment by the Holy Spirit, floating downward to where she could see Angela sitting on the bed. As Donna hovered near the ceiling, she realized that not only was she in Angela's apartment, but also that "her spirit went into the future. I see Angela sitting on the bed with her daughter, but Angela was told that she couldn't have no kids, okay? So, I see, I'm like wow, this is Angela," Donna thought excitedly, looking forward to returning to her body so that she could relieve Angela's anguish over her inability to have children.

"This is where it gets funny," Donna turned to me laughing. "I see myself back in my room. I'm like, okay. Let me get back in my body. I ain't getting back in my body. I hear the kids outside in the backyard, playing in the building, and I'm like, why ain't I getting in my body? At this point, I am freaking out. I'm like, I've been out of my body too long. Let me get back in my body. I don't hear no voices, no divine, no angels, no nothing. I'm just on my own. And I'm like, I'm out of my body too long. I've got to get back in my body. So then I panic. I'm falling on the floor. I said, 'Oh Lord, please Lord, please, just get me back in my body. Lord, please.' I'm begging. So all of a sudden no one's not saying nothing to me. So I said, 'Okay, Donna. Calm down. Just relax. God's in control. Relax.'

"So I get up off the floor on my knees, and I said, 'Okay, what do you want me to see?' So then, all of a sudden, I feel myself being pulled further into the future. So then, I go again into the future, but further into Angela's future. When I come in, I'm coming out of her bathroom. I walk to the right, and there's two playpens to the right. One has a little—one kid's sleeping in the other pen, and the other little kid's looking up at me, smiling. It looked like it was a house. It looked like she had a daycare. So, then I go into Angela's room, and Angela's sitting on the floor watching television. And Angela's not a big person. But in this vision, you could tell that she had put weight on. I see her husband. See, a lot was told to me in this vision. I see a man lying in the bed, and I sense that the man is her husband. So at the time that I met Angela, Angela was not married. She didn't have no husband. That's the first thing I picked up. In this [material] world, she can't have kids, but I see her girl. In this [material] world, she's not married, but I see her husband."

Donna then decided to continue to explore Angela's home. "I'm walking around still looking around, and all of a sudden, this little kid comes down the hall and sees me! He starts screaming, 'Mom!' I'm like, okay. It's time to go now. It's time to bring me back. And I'm like, I go to the little kid, and I said, 'You can see me!?'"

"He starts screaming," laughed Donna. "I said, 'Lord, it's really time for me to go back,'" at which point her spirit finally returned to her body. "I go, I wake up, I'm in my body. Every time that happens to me, I've got to pinch myself, hit it, and then I like touch myself. Okay, I'm back. And I woke up. I immediately called Angela before she left for Cuba, and I said, 'Angela, you're gonna have a daughter.' And she's like, 'What? Donna, you know I told you this.' I said, 'I'm telling you. You're gonna have a daughter, and you're gonna get married.' Four months later, after she returned from Cuba, she married a guy, and she sent an ultrasound picture on Facebook. She sent me a picture of an ultrasound, and the ultrasound was of a baby girl, and she named her Wonder. And to this day, Angela says she tells everybody that I said, 'You're gonna have a girl.' And keep in mind, when I saw Angela's daughter, she was a teenager. She was not a baby. She was a teenager. So, like I said, you have to discern.

It goes back to what I was saying earlier about discernment. I knew that, okay, I compared this world to that [spiritual] world. In this [spiritual] world, she has a daughter and a husband. This [physical] world, no daughter, no husband. So that is what I needed to relay back to Angela, you see?" Donna asked me with a tilt of her head. "That is what I need. That is what the Holy Spirit wanted me to see. So the nails and all that had nothing to do with it. It [the journey into the spirit world] was to tell Angela, 'Yes, you can. You're gonna have a kid, and you're gonna get married,' and these were the things that Angela wanted and that's what I was supposed to do, and I picked up on it. Yes, I did, I picked up on it. Thank you, God."

CROSSING OVER THE DEAD

Donna's spiritual warriorship also included caring for the dead, and not simply those who had died at the bottom of Boston's social ladder. The Holy Spirit also insisted that Donna tend to Americans more broadly, especially the souls of enslaved Africans and marginalized American Indians who historically had been relegated to what Sharon Patricia Holland refers to as "places reserved for the dead." Holland writes: "Perhaps the most revolutionary intervention into conversations at the margins of race, gender, and sexuality is to let the dead—those already denied a sustainable subjectivity—speak from the place that is familiar to them . . . from the place reserved for the dead. . . . Embracing the subjectivity of death allows marginalized peoples to speak about the unspoken—to name the places *within* and *without* their cultural milieu where, like Beloved, they have slipped between the cracks of language."[2]

Aware of Donna's ability to attend to those who have "slipped between the cracks of language," one of her god-sisters, Joanne, called her on the telephone from North Carolina one evening to ask for help with a family living on an American Indian reservation.

"Her kids are having a problem sleeping at night," explained Joanne, asking if Donna was willing to teleport through the spirit world to diagnose the root of the issue. But as Joanne prayed over the telephone, Donna's tongues suddenly began to flow from her lips.

"I turned around, we prayed, I'm on the phone, and I put her on speakerphone. You can hear my tongues through the phone, and she's praying, I'm praying." When Donna returned to her ordinary consciousness, she suggested that the two women meet again on the phone the following day, only this time she asked Joanne to be physically present in the family's house on the reservation.

"Donna, I'm here," confirmed Joanne the following day, when Donna picked up the phone. Donna asked her to light a handful of sage and to walk around the home, while Donna retreated to her war room in Roxbury, where she prayed and calmed her mind. That's when the Holy Spirit opened the window of Donna's consciousness and allowed her to flutter into the spirit world.

"Does she live at the end of the road?" Donna asked Joanne, as her ephemeral body stood on a dirt path in North Carolina.

"Yeah," Joanne confirmed on the other end of the line.

"I see my spirit self [at the end of the road]," confirmed Donna. "So I just want to make sure I'm going in the right direction." As Donna walked down the middle of the path toward the lone house, she became aware of the souls of dozens of American Indians around her.

"As I'm walking, I see spirits, Indians walking toward this house." When they reached the home together, "the whole room is full of them," uttered Donna in amazement. That's when she realized that the living inhabitants of this home were being disturbed by the restless energy of banished Indian souls.

"So I said to Joanne, 'It's for us to help them cross over.' So I told her to go to the house and open a window to make a path for them to come through out of the home." As Donna emanated her inner light in prayer within the spirit realm, she "looked up at the window and saw them going up, each one of their spirits turning into the twinkle of a star."

Donna was blown away by what she had seen, returning to her body soon after with a deep sense of accomplishment, knowing that she had allowed the dead to "speak from the place that is familiar to them." As Donna eased into bed for a good night's rest, however, she suddenly awoke in the spirit world again, only this time to observe the curious silhouette of an American Indian man standing in the doorway of her Roxbury bedroom.

"He didn't say anything. He was stone-faced. He had a feather in his hand. Now, not every spirit can come into my room. It's off limits. If you're not of good will, you can't enter into my room. So when it came into my room, I knew he was good. So I look at him. He comes in. He has these beige moccasins on his feet, he's all in beige. He has the feather coming out of his hair, and things hanging down [from his clothes]. He has the chest thing [poncho-style shirt] and his tribe colors. So he comes over to me, and he hands me a white feather, and he puts the white feather on me. It was a big old, long feather." As Donna peered at the beautiful feather, she intuited its spiritual meaning. It was a symbolic gesture of high esteem, honoring Donna's bravery for entering a "place reserved for the dead."

A few days later, Donna called the mother of the little girl who was having trouble sleeping and offered one final piece of advice. Remembering the colors of the Indian spirit's clothing, Donna advised:

"Get a dreamcatcher for your daughter. Make sure the dreamcatcher has the colors white, red, black, and yellow."

GATHERING SOULS OF BLACK FOLK

Donna entered other "places reserved for the dead," the most harrowing of which was a North Carolina plantation lingering with the presence of enslaved Africans. After buying her new home in North Carolina, Joanne called on Donna again.

"There's something going on in here," she relayed.

"Joanne, keep me on the phone and go into your living room," directed Donna, who was already preparing to slip out of her body to visit Joanne's home in the other world.

"Well, there's a [Black] husband and a wife there, but there are a lot of other spirits there. They're slaves," observed Donna once she bounced into the spirit realm of Joanne's living room. "But there is a white man who owned this house where you're living. It was a planation. The owner on that plantation is a racist white guy, and he's making the slaves stay bounded to the house, still ordering them, telling them what to do. You have to help them cross over. Open the door, and let the spirits leave."

For the following three days, Donna and Joanne worked tirelessly together to release the souls of Black folk from their status as property. "They were so scared. They still thought they were slaves. This white slave master carrying a whip, he kept them in the basement, still made them feel like they were slaves, even though they could see present-day Black people like me who were free."

Donna continued: "I told Joanne, when the heavens open up, you tell them to go. And that's what happened. They each floated up one by one like tiny spheres of light, and it was so beautiful. I was in tears, because we've been free for hundreds of years, and they were still in bondage." As I listened to Donna's sense of anguish and triumph as she described reclaiming of victims of slavery from America's "original sin," I couldn't help but think about my visit to Phillis Wheatley's memorial again. Such places were what Pierre Nora refers to as "sites of memory," places "where memory crystallizes and secretes itself."[3]

As Donna labored in this imaginative environment of memory, something astonishing occurred. Other slaves from surrounding plantations converged on Joanne's house, having learned of the Black woman escorting runaways up high.

"Slaves from other homes were just congregating at her house and crossing over," Donna remarked in awe. At the same time, while these other Black souls were escaping home, Donna and Joanne went to blows with the former white masters, pissed as they were by the freeing of their captives.

"And one thing we did battle was the white guy to get rid of him, a white spirit. And he left. He hasn't been back since," proclaimed Donna victoriously. And for some reason the spirits of a Black husband and wife, the ones who Donna first encountered in the home, decided to remain on the property as its guardians, rather than move into the light.

"Yeah, the husband and wife slaves weren't bad spirits," Donna explained. "As a matter of fact," she told Joanne, "they don't want to leave. They're there to protect you." Joanne's house has been peaceful ever since.

"EVERYBODY TALKING ABOUT HEAVEN AIN'T GOING THERE"

Donna had become adept at laboring in the spirit world on behalf of the dispossessed and exiled of American culture—living persons and once-born souls still living in the shadows of history.[4] She had fashioned a bridge of light between material and ethereal realms for the souls of American Indians and enslaved Africans to cross over. She lay in wait to conquer supernatural sexism and to destroy the unclean spirits of rapists and pedophiles, some of whom attacked girls in her own family. She prayed for Black boys haunted by the spirit of death in the American criminal justice system. And she traveled to past and future worlds to make the present more livable for Black women and children in the streets of Boston whose bodies were circumscribed by structural inequality. If anyone was "audacious, courageous, or willful" enough to confront the devil himself within the gates of hell, it was Ms. Donna Haskins.[5]

The evening she went, Donna fell asleep in the comfort of her own bed in Roxbury, only to find herself in the spirit realm, standing above a cliff overlooking a vast canyon of dark caves, each one leading to another in a confusing maze of interlocking tunnels. In the distant reaches of the canyon, down in the valley, she could see a dark figure sitting on a throne holding a headless torso, its brain rolling around on the ground. Staring at the grotesque figure on the throne, Donna audaciously opened her mouth. "You took my nephews from me! You tried to destroy my life! You tried to kill me!" she lambasted the figure, recalling how she too, like the headless torso, had her Black female body severed from her soul upon the throne of American inequality. "I'm taking it all back, all back!" she gave voice to her fury.

Then, given the immensity of it all, atop the canyon voicing her truth, Donna suddenly felt alone. But as she looked around at the vastness of this underworld, she felt a hand brush gently against hers. It was Jesus. "When you enter [the tunnel], I will cover you the whole time," he promised.

"I realized, in that moment," Donna remarked, "that Jesus was giving me a 'walk-through' of hell."

So under the protection of Jesus, Donna moved slowly down the dark canyon, into hell's labyrinth.

"Hell stinks, Onaje, and it has many levels." Donna contorted her nose.

After what seemed to be just a short time, Donna arrived at what she believed was hell's deepest level. As she looked around, above and behind her, she made out a gruesome sight: "people walking with chain-links of fire wrapped around their ankles and necks and wrists, and people being whipped with whips of fire. And if they cried out or tried to call out to God, they got pulverized even more," she said solemnly. "It got to the point where they were tortured so much, they submitted themselves to the demons, gave them full control over them. These people were from different centuries, which I could tell from their clothing, and they were being tormented without rest."

Donna further described the individuals she observed in hell: "However they lived when they were human, if they were ignorant, disrespectful, never happy while they were living, always complained about their lives, addicted to greed, to jealousy, racist, or whatever, it transcended into hell. If this person was racist when he was alive, he was racist in hell. I could spot the racists in hell easily, because they were yelling the N-word at me in a heartbeat," she noticed.

"These people hated the color black so bad that it rotted their spirits. In hell, your body turns into whatever you are thinking.

These racist people appeared so ugly and rotted. That's what got me. They couldn't hide it like they do here in the physical world. The look on their faces, you saw the whole image of who they really are. If I had to give it a name, I'd call it the spirit of hatred. In this physical world, we might call it racism, but over there, in the spirit realm, they see it as hatred."

After Donna observed the corrosive spirit of hate a while longer, the Holy Spirit guided her back up the many dimensions of this underworld to the surface where she could gain one last view of the thing on the throne in the middle of the valley.

"What was it?" I asked Donna.

It was a "thing, a horror I don't need to describe," she responded. "Describing it will give it glory, and I'm not trying to give it glory. God told me only to call it an entity, a thing."

However, Donna was willing to share something of what she saw. This entity was surrounded by an immense shadow and falling into this shadow were "specks of light. These specks of light were being sucked up, vacuumed into the shadow." And as Donna watched the sparkles of light disappear into the deep void, the Holy Spirit remarked:

"These are me. These are the souls that need to be saved."

"He was showing me how the thing was taking people's souls without their consent," she explained. "Whenever a soul became addicted to hatred, to racism, to greed, to envy, to money, it was this entity's path to take it, to take the soul. And that's what he did. He took it. And they were not going willingly. He was taking it as if it was his authority. This little speck of light was God," and now Donna fully understood her purpose: to take back what the devil stole.

WHAT IF YOU READ YOUR BOOK TO YOUR SUBJECT(S)? OR, ON METHODOLOGY

ake Back What the Devil Stole was near completion. More than four years had passed since the day I walked into Ms. Donna Haskins's apartment and she reprimanded me for asking whether to remove my shoes. For years we spent countless hours together, laughing, crying, listening, and healing. We had even visited a few local bookstores together to share her story. I'll never forget one of those occasions when she turned to a young man sitting in the audience and yelled, "Stop it, stop it right now!" and proceeded to speak in tongues in his direction. The room fell silent as the owner of the bookstore, the crowd, and I grew uncomfortable, while the young man, who wasn't doing anything visibly out of place, pointed to himself with a perplexed look on his face as if to say, "Me?"

"Yes, you," Donna replied sharply. "You know who I'm talking to. Cut it out!" I was beginning to feel embarrassed and thought I should step in to redirect the conversation, but then, just as quickly, Donna turned to the crowd with a smile. "Now, where was I?" she asked. "What?" I thought, as I sank back into my seat feeling a sense of relief. After the program ended, I made way over to Donna to ask why she had been so harsh on the guy.

"Onaje, I wasn't talking to him. I was talking to the demon behind him, the one he's carrying with him. I can't stand evil to be in my presence. It disgusts me!" "Oooooh," I said, finally comprehending the underlying meaning of her actions.

Even after all those years together, I was still capable of misinterpreting Donna's lived religion from the perspective of my own nagging empiricist scholarly bent, given my social location within a white male–dominated academy. By imposing my objectivist point of view onto Donna's behavior during this encounter, I had actually privileged my subjectivity over hers, effectively reducing her into an object of my own limited understanding. This positivist approach to Black women's knowledge, Patricia Hill Collins reminds us, often amounts to a form of violence. "Such criteria ask African-American women to objectify ourselves, [and] devalues our emotional life," Collins writes. My own discomfort at the bookstore was a critical reminder that in order to accurately convey the meaning of Donna's lived religion to the reader, her experience, her voice, her knowledge had to be centered throughout the manuscript. "Black feminist thought," Collins declares, "must be validated by ordinary African-American women who, in the words of Hannah Nelson, grow to womanhood 'in a world where the saner you are, the madder you are made to appear' (Gwaltney 1980, 7)."[1] This was certainly true for Donna. Just a few days after Donna's talk at the bookstore, the owner called me with troubling news. Something awful had just happened to the young man whom Donna had reprimanded earlier. I hung up the phone in silence. Donna had understood something after all.

As Clifford Geertz makes clear, ethnography is an act of interpretation.[2] We "read over the shoulders" of our subjects and hope to see the world as they see it, which means getting out of our own way, and working to acknowledge the cultural blinders we wear, habituated as we are to the different worlds we inhabit.

While there are of course limits to our ability to "know" and to "see" the world from the perspective of the people we hope to understand, we must at least find ways to avoid further silencing subjects, especially those who inhabit communities that have been historically marginalized by the work we do. For me, the methodological imperative to give voice to muted communities through ethnography, ultimately boils down to one important question—do my research subjects understand and assent to the monograph I write about them?

My field test for whether this is true is to actually read the monograph with my collaborators prior to publication. So on two cold days in December 2019, I flew to Boston and read the entire manuscript with Donna, word for word. Speaking to her over the phone days before my arrival, I could tell she was excited about my visit. Although we had collaborated for years to produce *Take Back What the Devil Stole*—through countless interviews, hours of participant-observation, family visits, field notes, coding the data, discussing theory, and more interviews—Donna left the writing to me. No doubt this was mostly because "access to literary practices is conditioned by wealth or poverty, geographical location . . . but also intrafamily relations," not to mention the fact that many of the supernatural encounters Donna experienced occurred in a realm irreducible to words.[3] So in my attempt to shift the imbalance of power that writing entails, we would listen to the words float off the page together and discuss the nearly finished product of our combined ethnographic labor.

DAY 1

When I finally walked into Donna's apartment on day 1, there was a pink sheet of paper on one of her bare walls behind her kitchen table that read "13 YEARS CANCER FREE. WE LOVE U NANA" in big black letters. Donna recently learned her cancer was still in remission and celebrated the news with family and friends. Everything else in the apartment was pretty much the same as the day I met her, except for the queen-sized mattress next to her mangled couch and another full-sized one near her front door. Both beds were there so that her youngest daughter and two granddaughters had a comfortable place to sleep whenever they spent the night.

Upon entering, I hugged Donna and sat down on her couch, while she thanked me for taking the time to visit. As usual, her beloved gray cat perched herself on the armrest near my left side, and her youngest daughter, Joy, said hello, as she lay on the mattress fiddling through her phone. I pulled out my laptop and opened the manuscript file. "Well, Donna, here's the book. Are you ready?" I asked, showing her the title page. Donna sat back on the couch with a nervous smile. "Well, go ahead Onaje!"

I was terrified. The first four chapters of the book offered a thick description of the horrors of Donna's coming of age as a young Black woman in the streets of Boston. Did she really want to relive those terrifying moments with me in print? There was something very public about the act of reading together. Our ethnography no longer felt like a private conversation between the two of us and the occasional spiritual presence who interjected itself into our interviews. Reading the words on the page meant that Donna's life had become public.

Before I began, I decided to explain my reasons for reading the book to her in the first place. "Donna, please stop me at any point if you don't understand something I've read, or if what I have said is incorrect. The contents of this book have to meet your approval and be validated by you. If there is something in here that you don't agree with, that is factually incorrect, or is not what you meant, we will take it out or correct it, okay?" I assured her. "Thank you so much, Onaje," she responded with obvious appreciation. "I really appreciate that, and don't worry, I'll let you know if something ain't right!" she declared. I was grateful. I hoped to convey to Donna that our collaboration didn't stop in the ethnographic field. I was inviting her to continue to create the text with me, to use her critical voice, and to ensure that the meaning of her experiences was accurately interpreted and conveyed through the act of writing.

Donna paid careful attention to each of my words as I began reading the introduction. "No, Jason said it like this," she corrected me several times, as I read her the passage describing her prophesying to Jason about his basketball aspirations. 'Okay, got it Donna. Thank you," I responded, as we corrected the manuscript in real time. And I found out later that she was also fact-checking what I said about myself in the text. "Smiley, the young man you spoke about in the introduction," Donna would tell me the following day when I returned to read the second half of the book. "I checked with my sister because she knows everyone over in Heath Street Projects, and you were right. She knew his name right away! She said he did used to be over there hanging out all the time." As much as I had been working as an ethnographer to independently verify the facts of Donna's story, she had been equally invested in interrogating the authenticity of my authorial presence in the text all along as well.

Donna exploded in laughter when I read about the first time we met. "You didn't know what hit you, did you?" she chuckled. And when I began reading about my observation of her entering into communication with unseen presences, she began thanking the Holy Spirit right away, in the middle of my reading. "Thank you, Holy Spirit," she repeated whenever a passage seemed pleasing not just to her but to the invisible presences listening alongside us. As we read deeper into the text, it became clearer to me that the simple act of reading the book to Donna had itself become a spiritual exercise. Not only had I encouraged her to take part in creating the text with me, but in doing so I had implicitly invited her spirits to join in the crafting as well. By reading the document together, we had openly and daringly placed the question of authorship at the center of our work.

For the following six to seven hours, we laughed and cried over the manuscript, and Donna's passions ran high each time I read a passage that expressed her voice with such accuracy that she could have written it herself. "That's me! That's me Onaje. Thank you for saying it the way I said it! You kept my words!" she exclaimed. And although she cried when I read passages that described the pain that led to her multiple suicide attempts, she also assured me, "These are tears of joy, Onaje. Don't worry, these are tears of joy." Donna had a look of peaceful vindication on her face as I read. The book itself was living proof that she had taken back what the devil stole. And now she felt honored that her life would become a gift to others. "I'm an open book, Onaje," she explained. "I made the decision, when we started this book, to tell the whole truth, to keep it real, and I kept it real, you hear me!"

The practice of reading the entire first section of the manuscript to Donna on that first day was exhausting, but I was relieved. Not only had she understood the text, which meant that this book would be accessible to other readers living in similarly marginalized social and cultural locations, but she also actively participated in ensuring that the text itself was an authentic expression of her voice and lived experience.

As I reached the final words of part 1, the sun had already ceased spying through Donna's window at my laptop. I closed the computer and turned to Donna, who seemed overwhelmed with emotion. Her facial expression reminded me of a similar moment a few weeks earlier when I had stopped by her apartment to read her a particularly powerful passage from the book. On that occasion, when I finished reading, she turned to me and began to weep. "Thank you, Onaje, for believing me," she cried. "Thank you for believing me. You never once questioned me. When everyone was saying I was crazy, people in my family, you always believed me. Thank you!" Donna broke down sobbing. She had indeed grown up in a world where the saner she was, the madder she looked. Her words broke open my heart. I hadn't fully understood what the act of listening and reading to her really meant until now. It meant that she was no longer invisible. It meant that she existed. It meant that Donna's life mattered.

DAY 2

I returned to Donna's apartment early in the morning on the second day, excited to read the second half of the book to her. I brought with me some of my favorite breakfast treats to share and wasted no time opening my computer. Donna sat down next to me with a huge smile on her face. "Now we are going to read about my spiritual battles, right? You have to make sure to get my battles right!" she insisted. "You will be the judge," I assured her.

The first section I read to Donna contained the passages describing her spiritual warfare against an incubus she referred to as the "spirit of lust." As I described her encounters with this demonic entity in vivid detail, she passionately cheered me on, "Yes, yes, that's exactly how he looked! Yes!" As I read further, Donna even began to predict what I would say next, especially if I was reading a passage that quoted her directly. And when I reached an event that she wanted to make absolute sure I portrayed it exactly as it happened, she would often beat me to the punch. "Onaje, now don't forget that when I went into the realm, I saw . . . ," she would say. "Don't worry Donna, I got it right here," I would respond quickly, pointing to the text. Actually, Donna's ability to recall her encounters in the spirit realm, in excruciating detail and often with profound emotional content, was one of the things that impressed me most about her. There were several occasions during interviews when I asked her to retell one of her stories because I wanted to make sure my notes were accurate. She never failed to describe the same exact event, including the minutest of details. Her retellings were often so vivid and emotionally charged that I began working hard to get her stories right the first time, thus sparing her the agony of reliving them over and over again.

At the same time, while Donna's memory of her supernatural experiences was exquisite, there were times when nailing down *when* a particular encounter in the spirit world occurred, in relation to her other spiritual encounters, became less clear. Given the fact that Donna spent so much time outside of her body and the nature of time itself in that realm, attempting to reduce all of her supernatural encounters into a chronological narrative was occasionally challenging. My solution to this dilemma was to keep the narrative framework whenever verifiable, thereby illustrating the stages of Donna's spiritual growth and evolving relationship with herself and the culture around her. However, when an event occurred in the spirit realm that eluded an exact chronological time, I organized it thematically, thereby giving the reader a sense of Donna's overall conception of similar such encounters.

As I came close to finishing reading the final section of the manuscript, I wondered what Donna's overall thoughts were about the decisions I had made in organizing the book. Up until that point she had found very few mistakes in the general narrative, and when she did, she stopped me quickly and we corrected it together. We had been reading the book together now for at least fourteen hours over two days, and it was gratifying to know that she felt the text accurately expressed her ever-evolving relationship to her environment and the spirit world. Toward the end, Donna was especially excited about the passages where I described her spiritual battles. When I read about the extraordinary courage angels displayed in their campaign to protect "God's children," she pumped her fist as if she were in the spirit realm fighting alongside them. And she was clearly touched to the bone when I read about her crossing over the souls of enslaved Africans and oppressed American Indians. "It was like those enslaved Black people were still feeling they were under white people on the other side!" she lamented.

When I finally reached the last sentence of the book, Donna and I sighed and turned to each other. "I'm not tired. Can you believe it?" I asked. "It's like something about reading this book to you all day has put me on a cloud," I exclaimed. "Do you know, I feel the same way," she observed, with a sense of surprise. "I expected to be exhausted. It's like ten o'clock in the evening and you been here all day, but I feel good!" Donna affirmed. It certainly felt like the shared practice of reading this book together had done something to nourish our bodies and souls. "So what did you think of the book?" I finally asked. "Are there any other errors or things still out of place that I need to correct?" A look of peace washed over Donna's face. "Onaje, this is the way the Holy Spirit wants it to be." And at those words, I closed my laptop. The Holy Spirit had seized the last word. Who then had authored the manuscript? I wondered. Me? Donna? The Holy Spirit? Given the extraordinary nature of the material itself, it was a messy question with no straightforward answers. But one thing was certain. This book was accessible to Ms. Donna Haskins, and she recognized her voice in the telling—and from the perspective of Black feminist thought, that was quintessential.

NOTES

INTRODUCTION

1. Onaje X. O. Woodbine, *Black Gods of the Asphalt: Religion, Hip Hop, and Street Basketball* (New York: Columbia University Press, 2016).
2. David D. Hall, ed., *Lived Religion in America: Toward a History of Practice* (Princeton, N.J.: Princeton University Press, 1997).
3. Nancy Tatom Ammerman, *Sacred Stories, Spiritual Tribes: Finding Religion in Everyday Life* (Oxford: Oxford University Press, 2013). Other notable research includes Nancy T. Ammerman, ed., *Everyday Religion: Observing Modern Religious Lives* (Oxford: Oxford University Press, 2007); and Meredith B. McGuire, *Lived Religion: Faith and Practice in Everyday Life* (Oxford: Oxford University Press, 2008).
4. Alice Walker coined the term "womanist" in her seminal work *In Search of Our Mothers' Gardens: Womanist Prose* (New York: Harcourt Brace Jovanovich, 1983). Emilie Townes describes Walker's four-part definition of "womanist" as containing the following elements: "tradition, community, self, and critique of white feminist thought." See Emilie M. Townes, "Ethics as an Art of Doing the Work Our Soul Must Have," in *Womanist Theological Ethics: A Reader*, ed. Katie Geneva Cannon, Emilie M. Townes, and Angela D. Sims (Louisville, Ky.: Westminster John Knox, 2011), 35.

    This section is greatly indebted to the work featured in Nancy Ammerman's article "Lived Religion," in *Emerging Trends in the Social and Behavioral Sciences: An Interdisciplinary, Searchable, and Linkable*

Resource, ed. Robert A. Scott and Stephen M. Kosslyn ([Hoboken, N.J.:] Wiley Online Library, 2015). Describing the unique contribution that the study of "lived religion" has made to the discipline of religious studies, Peter Berger writes: "Much of the sociology of religion has dealt either with the aforementioned institutions—that is, broadly speaking, with the internal condition and the societal role of churches—or with survey data covering the beliefs and behavior of large populations. Obviously, both procedures have yielded important insights. But what both have in common is remoteness from much of what constitutes the reality of religion in the lives of many people. . . . Much of religious life takes place outside these institutional locales." See Peter Berger, "Foreword," in Ammerman, *Everyday Religion*, v.

5. Anthony B. Pinn, "Watch the Body with New Eyes: Womanist Thought's Contribution to a Humanist Notion of Ritual," *Religious Encounters* 57, no. 3 (Fall 2007): 404.

6. Emilie M. Townes, *Womanist Ethics and the Cultural Production of Evil* (New York: Palgrave Macmillan, 2006), 3.

7. Townes, 23.

8. Tamura Lomax, *Jezebel Unhinged: Loosing the Black Female Body in Religion and Culture* (Durham, N.C.: Duke University Press, 2018), 21.

9. See Hortense J. Spillers, "Mama's Baby, Papa's Maybe: An American Grammar Book," *Diacritics* 17, no. 2 (Summer 1987): 67. Spillers says of the enslavement of people of African descent in the Americas: "First of all, their New-World, diasporic plight marked a *theft of the body*—a willful and violent (and unimaginable from this distance) severing of the captive body from its motive will, its active desire."

10. Spillers, 65.

11. See Anthony Pinn, "Black Bodies in Pain and Ecstasy: Terror, Subjectivity, and the Nature of Black Religion," *Nova Religio: The Journal of Alternative and Emergent Religions* 7, no. 1 (July 2003): 77–79. Pinn suggests that "the story of black religion is one of resistance to this objectification, a wrestling with history through which black subjectivity was asserted and black bodies reclaimed."

12. See Charles H. Long, *Significations: Signs, Symbols, and Images in the Interpretation of Religion* (Aurora, Colo.: Davies Group of Publishers,

1999). W. E. B. Du Bois makes a similar argument in *The Souls of Black Folk* (Chicago: McClurg, 1903), 2: "The Negro," he says, lives in "a world which yields them no true self-consciousness, but only lets him see himself through the revelation of the other world."

13. Rudolf Otto, *The Idea of the Holy*, trans. John Harvey (Oxford: Oxford University Press, 1958), 29.

14. Long, *Significations*, 177.

15. John R. Logan and Brian Stults, "The Persistence of Segregation in the Metropolis: New Findings from the 2010 Census," Census Brief prepared for Project US2010 (2011), https://s4.ad.brown.edu/Projects /Diversity/Data/Report/report2.pdf.

16. METCO formally refers to the Metropolitan Council for Educational Opportunity. See https://metcoinc.org.

17. D. W. Winnicott, *Playing and Reality* (New York: Routledge, 1991), 103 (italics mine). For a clear analysis of Winnicott's definition of this third area of human experience, see W. W. Meissner, *Life and Faith: Psychological Perspectives and Religious Experience* (Washington, D.C.: Georgetown University Press, 1987), xiii. Meissner writes: "Winnicott (1971) had staked a claim for an intermediate area of experience, the area of illusion, which was neither exclusively subjective nor objective but was in some degree both. This middle ground, which he referred to in terms of 'transitional phenomena' or area of illusion, was the realm in which illusion and reality not only touched but became inextricably intermingled."

18. Townes, *Womanist Ethics*, 19–20.

19. Janice Radway, Foreword, in Avery F. Gordon, *Ghostly Matters: Haunting and the Sociological Imagination* (Minneapolis: University of Minnesota Press, 2008), ix.

20. For a comprehensive study of Yoruba religion in Africa and in the Americas, see Terry Rey and Jacob K. Olupona, eds., *Òrìsà Devotion as World Religion: The Globalization of Yoruba Religious Culture* (Madison: University of Wisconsin Press, 2009).

21. For an excellent examination of inequality and the imposter phenomenon among faculty of color in higher education, see T. Elon Dancy II and Jean-Marie Gaetane, "Faculty of Color in Higher Education: Exploring the Intersections of Identity, Impostership, and Internalized

Racism," *Mentoring and Tutoring: Partnership in Learning* 22, no. 4 (214): 354–72.

22. ESV Genesis 2:9.

23. See Zora Neale Hurston, *Mules and Men* (New York: Amistad, 2008).

24. Urie Bronfenbrenner, *The Ecology of Human Development: Experiments by Nature and Design* (Cambridge, Mass.: Harvard University Press, 1981).

25. Gordon, *Ghostly Matters*, 3.

1. "THE DEVIL HAD HIS WAY WITH ME"

1. Jane Roessner, *A Decent Place to Live: From Columbia Point to Harbor Point—a Community History* (Boston: Northeastern University Press, 2000), 17–18.

2. Roessner, 21.

3. Roessner, 72.

4. On social death, see Orlando Patterson, *Slavery and Social Death: A Comparative Study* (Cambridge, Mass.: Harvard University Press, 1982), 38.

5. See Matthew 3:11 where John the Baptist proclaims: "I indeed baptize you with water unto repentance: but he that cometh after me is mightier than I, whose shoes I am not worthy to bear: he shall baptize you with the Holy Ghost, and with fire." Speaking of initiatory ordeals that call one to serve the spirit, African shaman Malidoma Patrice Some writes: "Calls to duty are not interested in your prior plans, not to mention your opinion, and do not come with the kind of umbrella of safety one would naturally want in the interest of predictability and comfort. . . . In these moments of dismantling, one cannot see the light. Initiation is a brush with uncertainty, danger, and death." See Malidoma Patrice Some, "Foreword," in John Lockley, *Leopard Warrior: A Journey Into the African Teachings of Ancestry, Instinct, and Dreams* (Louisville, Ky.: Sounds True, 2017), ix–x.

6. Avery F. Gordon, *Ghostly Matters: Haunting and the Sociological Imagination* (Minneapolis: University of Minnesota Press, 2008), 3.

7. Tamura Lomax, *Jezebel Unhinged: Loosing the Black Female Body in Religion and Culture* (Durham, N.C.: Duke University Press, 2018), xiii.

8. Lomax, 14.
9. National Sexual Violence Resource Center, "Statistics About Sexual Violence," from https://www.nsvrc.org/sites/default/files/publications _nsvrc_factsheet_media-packet_statistics-about-sexual-violence_0 .pdf.
10. Thema Bryant-Davis et al., "Struggling to Survive: Sexual Assault, Poverty, and Mental Health Outcomes of African American Women," *American Journal of Orthopsychiatry* 80, no. 1 (January 2010): 62.
11. For an excellent study that provides historical context for the Boston busing crisis, see Zebulon Vance Miletsky, "Before Busing: Boston's Long Movement for Civil Rights and the Legacy of Jim Crow in the 'Cradle of Liberty,'" *Journal of Urban History* 43, no. 2 (February 2017): 204–17.
12. See Joy DeGruy Leary, *Post Traumatic Slave Syndrome: America's Legacy of Enduring Injury and Healing* (Milwaukee: Uptone, 2005).
13. A recent *New York Times* article reports that "African-Americans are 75 percent more likely than others to live near facilities that produce hazardous waste." See Linda Villarosa, "Pollution Is Killing Black Americans. This Community Fought Back," *New York Times*, July 28, 2020.
14. See Elaine Bell Kaplan, *Not Our Kind of Girl: Unraveling the Myths of Black Teenage Motherhood* (Berkeley: University of California Press, 1997).
15. Bryant-Davis et al., "Struggling," 63.
16. Marvin Gaye, "Let's Get It On," *Let's Get It On*, Motown Records, 1973, CD.

2. "I REALLY DIDN'T WANT TO GIVE UP MY KID"

1. Esther J. Jenkins, "Black Women and Community Violence: Trauma, Grief, and Coping," *Women and Therapy* 25, no. 3–4 (2002): 35.
2. See Gillian Eagle and Debra Kaminer, "Continuous Traumatic Stress: Expanding the Lexicon of Traumatic Stress," *Peace and Conflict: Journal of Peace Psychology* 19, no. 2 (May 2013): 85–99. The authors write: "We propose *continuous traumatic stress* (CTS) as a supplementary

construct within the lexicon of traumatic stress, to describe the experience and impact of living in contexts of realistic current and ongoing danger, such as protracted political or civil conflict or pervasive community violence."

3. Toni Morrison, *Beloved* (New York: Vintage, 2004).

4. W. W. Meissner, *Freud and Psychoanalysis* (Notre Dame, Ind.: University of Notre Dame Press, 2000), 200.

5. D. W. Winnicott writes: "This intermediate area of experience, unchallenged in respect of its belonging to inner or external (shared) reality, constitutes the greater part of the infant's experience, and throughout life is retained in the intense experiencing that belongs to the arts and to religion and to imaginative living, and to creative scientific work." See D. W. Winnicott, *Playing and Reality* (New York: Routledge, 1991), 14.

6. Solimar Otero, "Residual Transcriptions: Ruth Landes and the Archive of Conjure," *Transforming Anthropology* 26, no. 1 (March 25, 2018): 5.

7. This explanation comes from my mentor and friend Chief Awodele Ifayemi, the Atunwase Awo of Ilobu Land in Nigeria, West Africa.

3. "AM I EVER GOING TO BE NORMAL?"

1. Kimberle Crenshaw, Priscilla Ocen, and Jyoti Nanda, *Black Girls Matter: Pushed Out, Overpoliced, and Underprotected* (New York: African American Policy Forum, Center for Intersectionality and Social Policy Studies, 2016).

2. Ralph Ellison, *Invisible Man* (New York: Vintage, 1995).

3. Describing the racial inequalities that are embedded in Boston's public school system and the difficulties of city has faced in overcoming them, Chungmei Lee writes: "Since the 1970's, it has been the City of Boston, rather than the metropolitan area as a whole, that has been the primary center of conflict for desegregation efforts. Boston's urban desegregation experience was, in important respects, the nation's worst, due to the unique level of violence and political polarization in the city." In Boston, Lee continues, "By 1973, the average black attended a school that was just 21 percent white, when total district enrollment was 57 percent white. . . . After decades of decreasing white enrollment,

as more and more white families moved out to suburbs, the average black student in Boston now attends a school that is 11 percent white in a school district that is 15 percent white." Chungmei Lee, "Racial Segregation and Educational Outcomes in Metropolitan Boston," The Civil Rights Project: Harvard University (April 2004), 5, 10, https://www.civilrightsproject.ucla.edu/research/metro-and-regional -inequalities/metro-boston-equity-initiative-1/racial-segregation-and -educational-outcomes-in-metropolitan-boston/Lee-Segregation -Educational-Outcomes-2004.pdf.

4. Malidoma Patrice Some, *Of Water and Spirit: Ritual, Magic, and Initiation in the Life of an African Shaman* (New York: Penguin, 1995), 8.

5. See Sebastian Gunther, "Muhammad, the Illiterate Prophet: An Islamic Creed in the Qur'an and Qur'anic Exegesis," *Journal of Quranic Studies* 4, no. 1 (2002): 1–26.

6. Describing the goals or "diploma" of traditional education within his Dagara community, African shaman Malidoma Some writes: "Traditional education consists of three parts: enlargement of one's ability to see, destabilization of the body's habit of being bound to one's plane of being, and the ability to voyage transdimensionally and return." Some, *Of Water and Spirit*, 226. These abilities are precisely what Donna aims to acquire as she gains access to knowledge of what we might refer to as the supernatural.

4. "EVERY TIME YOU LEAVE, YOU TAKE A PIECE OF ME"

1. See American Cancer Society, *Cancer Facts and Figures for African Americans, 2019–2021* (Atlanta: American Cancer Society, 2019), 1.

2. Carlene Davis, "Stealing Love on the Side," *Sonic Sounds*, 1981, vinyl.

3. Earth, Wind, and Fire, "Reasons," *That's the Way of the World*, Legacy, 1975, vinyl.

4. Frankie Vallie, "Can't Take My Eyes Off You," *Solo*, Mercury, 1967, vinyl.

5. Yolanda Adams, "The Battle Is the Lord's," *Save the World*, Sony Legacy, 1997, CD.

6. For an excellent analysis of the musical nature of black preaching, see James Weldon Johnson, *God's Trombones: Seven Negro Sermons in Verse* (London: Penguin Classics, 2008).

7. See Theodore M. Vial, "Friedrich Schleiermacher on the Central Place of Worship in Theology," *Harvard Theological Review* 91, no. 1 (January 1998): 68. Vial writes: "DeVries argues that preaching, for Schleiermacher, is an incarnational event. In other words, it is in preaching that the picture of Christ is represented and thus confronts and affects hearers in precisely the same way that Jesus' followers were confronted with his perfect God-consciousness; this is the origin of Christian faith." For further explanation, see Dawn DeVries, *Jesus Christ in the Preaching of Calvin and Schleiermacher* (Louisville, Ky.: Westminster John Knox, 1996).

5. INCUBUS

1. Dianne M. Stewart, "Womanist Theology in the Caribbean Context: Critiquing Culture, Rethinking Doctrine, and Expanding Boundaries," *Journal of Feminist Studies in Religion* 20, no. 1 (Spring 2004): 75, 77. Stewart writes: "Yet, while incarnation may be valid for Christians in its christological focus, it is important to remember that, for the BaKongo, their Kumina descendants in Jamaica, and other African-derived religious communities in the diaspora, incarnation is the recurring event of embodied Deity/ancestor made manifest in possession trance. It is most probably that this incarnational emphasis in African religion provided a theological strainer, if you will, an aesthetic and discriminating theological device through which a majority of enslaved Africans filtered Christian symbols and religious ideas. Consequently, what emerged in the formation of both African-derived religions and black North American Christian traditions was an emphasis on the Spirit (pneumatology)."

2. C. W. Ruth, *The Second Work of Grace* (Weldon Spring, Mo.: Pentecostal, 1920), 7–8.

6. SEEDS OF EVIL

1. Yolanda Adams, "I'm Gonna Be Ready," *Believe*, Elektra Entertainment 2001, CD.

2. See Kelly M. Hoffman et al., "Racial Bias in Pain Assessment and Treatment Recommendations, and False Beliefs About Biological Differences Between Blacks and Whites," *PNAS* 113, no. 16 (April 2016): 4296–4301.

7. CHRYSALIS

1. Donna was referring to Matthew 14:25–29: "Shortly before dawn Jesus went out to them, walking on the lake. When the disciples saw him walking on the lake, they were terrified. 'It's a ghost,' they said, and cried out in fear. But Jesus immediately said to them: 'Take courage! It is I. Don't be afraid.' 'Lord, if it is you,' Peter replied, 'tell me to come to you on the water.' 'Come,' he said. Then Peter got down out of the boat, walked on the water and came toward Jesus."
2. C. W. Ruth, *The Second Work of Grace* (Weldon Spring, Mo.: Pentecostal, 1920), 5, 8–9.
3. Donna was referring to Genesis 17:5: "No longer will you be called Abram; your name will be Abraham, for I have made you a father of many nations."
4. John 8:12.

8. BETWEEN WORLDS

1. Donna was referring to Matthew 4: "Then Jesus was led by the Spirit into the wilderness to be tempted by the devil."
2. See Toni Morrison, *Beloved* (New York: Vintage, 2004), 244. Also see Onaje X. O. Woodbine, *Black Gods of the Asphalt: Religion, Hip Hop, and Street Basketball* (New York: Columbia University Press, 2016), 146.
3. Janice Radway, "Foreword," in Avery F. Gordon, *Ghostly Matters: Haunting and the Sociological Imagination* (Minneapolis: University of Minnesota Press, 2008), viii.

9. TREASURES FROM HEAVEN

1. See "The West Tennessee Historical Society Papers," *West Tennessee Historical Society* 56 (2002): 41. "Pentecostalism had roots in the holiness movement of the late nineteenth century. The holiness movement embraced the Wesleyan doctrine of 'sanctification' or the second work

of grace, subsequent to conversion. Pentecostalism added a third work of grace, called the baptism of the Holy Ghost, which is often accompanied by glossolalia." Also see Vinson Synan, *The Holiness-Pentecostal Tradition: Charismatic Movements in the Twentieth Century* (Grand Rapids, Mich.: Eerdmans, 1997).

2. See Isaiah 55:9. "As the heavens are higher than the earth, so are my ways higher than your ways and my thoughts than your thoughts."

3. See Proverbs 3:5: "Trust the Lord with all your heart and lean not on your own understanding."

4. I have borrowed this connection between flying and dreams of the oppressed from Kareem Abdul-Jabbar, who says: "When it's played the way it's supposed to be played, basketball happens in the air, flying, floating, elevated above the floor, levitating, the way oppressed peoples of this earth imagine themselves in their dreams." *On the Shoulders of Giants*, directed by Deborah Morales (Union Productions, 2011), DVD.

10. THE DEVIL IS A LIAR

1. The quote is from Emilie M. Townes, *Womanist Ethics and the Cultural Production of Evil* (New York: Palgrave Macmillan, 2006), 3.

2. Sharon Patricia Holland, *Raising the Dead: Readings of Death and (Black) Subjectivity* (Durham, N.C.: Duke University Press, 2000), 4–5.

3. Pierre Nora, "Between Memory and History: Les Lieux de Mémoire," *Representations* no. 26 (Spring 1989): 7.

4. For an excellent analysis of the meaning of the quote in the heading, which comes from a Negro spiritual, see Howard Thurman, *Deep River: The Negro Spiritual Speaks of Life and Death* (Richmond, Ind.: Friends United, 1975), 36–38. Thurman writes: "The setting of this spiritual is very dramatic. The slave had often heard his master's minister talk about heaven, the final abode of the righteous. . . . He reasoned, 'There must be two separate heavens—no, this could not be true, because there is only one God. God cannot be divided in this way. I have it! I am having my hell now—when I die I shall have my heaven. The master is having his heaven now; when he dies he will have his hell.'"

5. Here, in describing Donna's character, I am making reference to the first part of Alice Walker's definition of the term "womanist": "'You acting womanish,' i.e., like a woman. Usually referring to outrageous, audacious, courageous or *willful* behavior. Wanting to know more and in greater depth than is considered 'good' for one. . . . Responsible. In charge. Serious." Alice Walker, *In Search of Our Mother's Gardens: Womanist Prose* (New York: Harcourt Brace Jovanovich, 1983), xi.

WHAT IF YOU READ YOUR BOOK TO YOUR SUBJECT(S)?

1. Patricia Hill Collins, *Black Feminist Thought: Knowledge, Consciousness, and the Politics of Empowerment* (Routledge: New York, 2000), 266.
2. Clifford Geertz writes, "The culture of a people is an ensemble of texts, themselves ensembles, which the anthropologist strains to read over the shoulders of those to whom they properly belong." Clifford Geertz, "Deep Play: Notes on the Balinese Cockfight," in *The Interpretation of Cultures* (New York: Basic Books, 2017), 473.
3. Katherine E. Hoffman, "Culture as Text: Hazards and Possibilities of Geertz's Literary/Literacy Metaphor," *Journal of North African Studies* 14, nos. 3/4 (September/December, 2009): 418.

BIBLIOGRAPHY

American Cancer Society. *Cancer Facts and Figures for African Americans, 2019–2021.* Atlanta: American Cancer Society, 2019.

Ammerman, Nancy Tatom. *Everyday Religion: Observing Modern Religious Lives.* Oxford: Oxford University Press, 2007.

——. "Lived Religion." In *Emerging Trends in the Social and Behavioral Sciences: An Interdisciplinary, Searchable, and Linkable Resource,* ed. Robert A. Scott and Stephen M. Kosslyn. [Hoboken, N.J.:] Wiley Online Library, 2015.

——. *Sacred Stories, Spiritual Tribes: Finding Religion in Everyday Life.* Oxford: Oxford University Press, 2013.

Bourdieu, Pierre. *The Weight of the World: Social Suffering in Contemporary Society.* Stanford, Calif.: Stanford University Press, 2000.

Bronfenbrenner, Urie. *The Ecology of Human Development: Experiments by Nature and Design.* Cambridge, Mass.: Harvard University Press, 1981.

Brown, Karen McCarthy. *Mama Lola: A Vodou Priestess in Brooklyn.* Los Angeles: University of California Press, 2010.

Bryant-Davis, Thema, Sarah E. Ullman, Yuying Tsong, Shaquita Tillman, and Kimberly Smith. "Struggling to Survive: Sexual Assault, Poverty, and Mental Health Outcomes of African American Women." *American Journal of Orthopsychiatry* 80, no. 1 (January 2010): 61–70.

Cannon, Katie Geneva, Emilie M. Townes, and Angela D. Sims, eds. *Womanist Theological Ethics: A Reader.* Louisville, Ky: Westminster John Knox, 2011.

Clifford, James, and George E. Marcus, eds. *Writing Culture: The Poetics and Politics of Ethnography*. Los Angeles: University of California Press, 1986.

Collins, Patricia Hill. *Black Feminist Thought: Knowledge, Consciousness, and the Politics of Empowerment*. New York: Routledge, 2000.

Crenshaw, Kimberle, Priscilla Ocen, and Jyoti Nanda. *Black Girls Matter: Pushed Out, Overpoliced, and Underprotected*. New York: African American Policy Forum, Center for Intersectionality and Social Policy Studies, 2016.

DeVries, Dawn. *Jesus Christ in the Preaching of Calvin and Schleiermacher*. Louisville, Ky.: Westminster John Knox, 1996.

Du Bois, W. E. B. *The Souls of Black Folk*. Chicago: McClurg, 1903.

Eagle, Gillian, and Debra Kaminer. "Continuous Traumatic Stress: Expanding the Lexicon of Traumatic Stress." *Peace and Conflict: Journal of Peace Psychology* 19, no. 2 (May 2013): 85–99.

Ellison, Ralph. *Invisible Man*. New York: Vintage, 1995.

Geertz, Clifford. "Deep Play: Notes on the Balinese Cockfight." In *The Interpretation of Cultures*. New York: Basic Books, 2017.

——. *The Interpretations of Cultures*. New York: Basic Books, 2017.

Gordon, Avery F. *Ghostly Matters: Haunting and the Sociological Imagination*. Minneapolis: University of Minnesota Press, 2008.

Gunther, Sebastian. "Muhammad, the Illiterate Prophet: An Islamic Creed in the Qur'an and Qur'anic Exegesis." *Journal of Quranic Studies* 4, no. 1 (2002): 1–26.

Hall, David D., ed. *Lived Religion in America: Toward a History of Practice*. Princeton, N.J.: Princeton University Press, 1997.

Hoffman, Katherine E. "Culture as Text: Hazards and Possibilities of Geertz's Literary/Literacy Metaphor." *Journal of North African Studies* 14, nos. 3/4 (September/December 2009): 417–30.

Hoffman, Kelly M., Sophie Trawalter, Jordan R. Axt, and M. Norman Oliver. "Racial Bias in Pain Assessment and Treatment Recommendations, and False Beliefs About Biological Differences Between Blacks and Whites." *PNAS* 113, no. 16 (April 2016): 4296–301.

Holland, Sharon Patricia. *Raising the Dead: Readings of Death and (Black) Subjectivity*. Durham, N.C.: Duke University Press, 2000.

Hurston, Zora Neale. *Mules and Men*. New York: Amistad, 2008.

——. *Their Eyes Were Watching God*. New York: Harper Perennial Modern Classics, 2006.

Jenkins, Esther J. "Black Women and Community Violence: Trauma, Grief, and Coping." *Women and Therapy* 25, no. 3–4 (2002): 29–44.

Johnson, James Weldon. *God's Trombones: Seven Negro Sermons in Verse.* London: Penguin Classics, 2008.

Kaplan, Elaine Bell. *Not Our Kind of Girl: Unraveling the Myths of Black Teenage Motherhood.* Berkeley: University of California Press, 1997.

Leary, Joy DeGruy. *Post Traumatic Slave Syndrome: America's Legacy of Enduring Injury and Healing.* Milwaukee, Wis.: Uptone Press, 2005.

Lee, Chungmei. "Racial Segregation and Educational Outcomes in Metropolitan Boston." The Civil Rights Project: Harvard University, April 2004. https://www.civilrightsproject.ucla.edu/research/metro-and-regio nal-inequalities/metro-boston-equity-initiative-1/racial-segregation -and-educational-outcomes-in-metropolitan-boston/Lee-Segregation -Educational-Outcomes-2004.pdf.

Lockley, John. *Leopard Warrior: A Journey Into the African Teachings of Ancestry, Instinct, and Dreams.* Louisville, Ky.: Sounds True, 2017.

Lomax, Tamura. *Jezebel Unhinged: Loosing the Black Female Body in Religion and Culture.* Durham, N.C.: Duke University Press, 2018.

Long, Charles H. *Significations: Signs, Symbols, and Images in the Interpretation of Religion.* Aurora, Colo.: Davies Group, 1999.

McGuire, Meredith B. *Lived Religion: Faith and Practice in Everyday Life.* Oxford: Oxford University Press, 2008.

Meissner, W. W. *Freud and Psychoanalysis.* Notre Dame, Ind.: University of Notre Dame Press, 2000.

——. *Life and Faith: Psychological Perspectives and Religious Experience.* Washington, D.C.: Georgetown University Press, 1987.

Miletsky, Zebulon Vance. "Before Busing: Boston's Long Movement for Civil Rights and the Legacy of Jim Crow in the 'Cradle of Liberty.'" *Journal of Urban History* 43, no. 2 (February 2017): 204–17.

Morrison, Toni. *Beloved.* New York: Vintage, 2004.

Nora, Pierre. "Between Memory and History: Les Lieux de Mémoire," *Representations*, no. 26 (Spring 1989): 7–24.

Otero, Solimar. *Archives of Conjure: Stories of the Dead in Afrolatinx Cultures.* New York: Columbia University Press, 2020.

——. "Residual Transcriptions: Ruth Landes and the Archive of Conjure." *Transforming Anthropology* 26, no. 1 (March 2018): 3–17.

Otto, Rudolf. *The Idea of the Holy*. Trans. John Harvey. Oxford: Oxford University Press, 1958.

Patterson, Orlando. *Slavery and Social Death: A Comparative Study*. Cambridge, Mass.: Harvard University Press, 1982.

Pinn, Anthony B. "Black Bodies in Pain and Ecstasy: Terror, Subjectivity, and the Nature of Black Religion." *Nova Religio: The Journal of Alternative and Emergent Religions* 7, no. 1 (July 2003): 76–89.

——. "Watch the Body with New Eyes: Womanist Thought's Contribution to a Humanist Notion of Ritual." *Religious Encounters* 57, no. 3 (Fall 2007): 404–11.

Plato. *The Republic*. Trans. Allan Bloom. New York: Basic Books, 2013.

Rey, Terry, and Jacob K. Olupona, eds. *Òrìsà Devotion as World Religion: The Globalization of Yoruba Religious Culture*. Madison: University of Wisconsin Press: 2009.

Roessner, Jane. *A Decent Place to Live: From Columbia Point to Harbor Point—A Community History*. Boston: Northeastern University Press, 2000.

Ruth, C. W. *The Second Work of Grace*. Weldon Spring, Mo.: Pentecostal, 1920.

Some, Malidoma Patrice. *Of Water and Spirit: Ritual, Magic and Initiation in the Life of an African Shaman*. New York: Penguin, 1995.

Spillers, Hortense J. "Mama's Baby, Papa's Maybe: An American Grammar Book." *Diacritics* 17, no. 2 (Summer 1987): 64–81.

Stewart, Dianne M. "Womanist Theology in the Caribbean Context: Critiquing Culture, Rethinking Doctrine, and Expanding Boundaries." *Journal of Feminist Studies in Religion* 20, no. 1 (Spring 2004): 61–82.

Synan, Vinson. *The Holiness-Pentecostal Tradition: Charismatic Movements in the Twentieth Century*. Grand Rapids, Mich.: Eerdmans, 1997.

Thurman, Howard. *Deep River: The Negro Spiritual Speaks of Life and Death*. Richmond, Ind.: Friends United Press, 1975.

Townes, Emilie M. *Womanist Ethics and the Cultural Production of Evil*. New York: Palgrave Macmillan, 2006.

Vial, Theodore M. "Friedrich Schleiermacher on the Central Place of Worship in Theology." *Harvard Theological Review* 91, no. 1 (January 1998): 59–73.

Villarosa, Linda. "Pollution Is Killing Black Americans. This Community Fought Back." *New York Times*, July 28, 2020.

Walker, Alice. *In Search of Our Mothers' Gardens: Womanist Prose*. New York: Harcourt Brace Jovanovich, 1983.

"The West Tennessee Historical Society Papers," *West Tennessee Historical Society* 56 (2002).

Wheatley, Phillis. *Poems on Various Subjects, Religious and Moral*. Denver: W. H. Lawrence, 1887.

Winnicott, D. W. *Playing and Reality*. New York: Routledge, 1991.

——. "Transitional Objects and Transitional Phenomena." *International Journal of Psychoanalysis* 34 (1953): 89–97.

Woodbine, Onaje X. O. *Black Gods of the Asphalt: Religion, Hip Hop, and Street Basketball*. New York: Columbia University Press, 2016.

INDEX

Abdul-Jabbar, Kareem, 240*n*4
African ancestors, 12–14, 185–86
African traditions, 15, 63, 237*n*6, 238*n*1
American Indians, 212–15
Ammerman, Nancy, 3–4
ancestors, 12–14, 185–86
angels, 15–16, 174–75, 183–85, 189, 190
archives of conjure, 62

basketball, 1–3, 8, 240*n*4
Beloved (Morrison), 62, 163, 212
Berger, Peter, 232*n*4
Bible, 234*n*5, 239*n*1, 239*n*3; and demons, 128, 191; Donna's study of, 120, 124, 128, 169, 179–80
Black experience: cancer, 90; and education, 65, 69, 236–37*n*3; and hazardous waste exposure, 235*n*13; health care, 142; and inexpressible, 6, 233*n*12; and resistance, 232*n*11. *See also* Black female oppression; inner city environment

Black female oppression: and education, 65; impact on author, 198–99; and positivist interpretation, 222; stereotypes, 4; and suicide attempts, 47–48; and trauma, 60–61, 235–36*n*2. *See also* sexual violence
Black Gods of the Asphalt (Woodbine), 3
body: enslavement as theft of, 232*n*9; and incarnation, 119–20; and lived religion, 4. *See also* sexual violence
Borders, John, III, 110–11, 124
Boston. *See* inner city environment
Bronfenbrenner, Urie, 18

Cannon, Katie, 4
Catholicism: and abortion, 52, 80, 87, 88; and angels, 182–83; and Donna's Baptist church experience, 109, 110, 111–12, 124; and Donna's mother, 41, 42, 80; and sexuality, 41, 126

Lightning Source UK Ltd.
Milton Keynes UK
UKHW022050211022
410881UK00006B/375